A READER'S GUIDE TO T. S. ELIOT

Other titles in the Reader's Guide Series

A Reader's Guide To

T. S. ELIOT

A POEM-BY-POEM ANALYSIS

BY GEORGE WILLIAMSON

Syracuse University Press

VVVVVVVVVVVVVVVVVVVVVVVVVVVVVVVVVVV

First Syracuse University Press Edition 1998

       02 03   6 5 4 3

Originally published in 1953. Reprinted by arrangement with Farrar, Straus & Giroux, Inc.

The paper used in this publication meets the minimum requirements of American National Standard for Information Sciences—Permanence of Paper for Printed Library Materials, ANSI Z39.48-1984. ∞™

Library of Congress Cataloging-in-Publication Data

Williamson, George, 1898–1968.
     A reader's guide to T. S. Eliot : a poem-by-poem analysis / by George Williamson. — 1st Syracuse University Press ed.
         p.   cm.
     Originally published : New York : Noonday, 1953.
     Includes bibliographical references (p.   ) and index.
     ISBN 0-8156-0500-5 (pbk. : alk. paper)
     1. Eliot, T. S. (Thomas Stearns), 1888–1965—Criticism and interpretation—Handbooks, manuals, etc.   I. Title
PS3509. L43Z898   1998
821'.912—dc21   97-43467

Manufactured in the United States of America

PREFATORY NOTE

This book should be read in company with Eliot's *Collected Poems* and *Four Quartets,* for it is primarily a guide to his poems, intended to open passages for the reader to explore. If some readers find the exposition inclined to the obvious, so much the better. Doubtless I have converted the substance of others to my own use; some of the debts are identified in text or bibliography, but many are beyond restoration. My largest creditors, however, are the students who have taken English 365 at the University of Chicago.

G. W.

May 1949

ACKNOWLEDGMENTS

For permission to quote from works of T. S. Eliot grateful thanks are due the author and these publishers: Methuen and Company, and Harcourt, Brace and Company, for *The Sacred Wood;* Faber and Faber, and Harcourt, Brace and Company, for *Selected Essays, Collected Poems, Four Quartets,* and the preface to *Anabasis;* Faber and Faber for the prefaces to *This American World* and *Ezra Pound: Selected Poems;* Faber and Faber, and Harvard University Press, for *The Use of Poetry and the Use of Criticism.* The section on *The Waste Land* is reprinted by permission from *Modern Philology.*

CONTENTS

"The sense is as the life and soul of language, without which all words are dead. Sense is wrought out of experience, the knowledge of human life and actions, or of the liberal arts."

Ben Jonson

Chapter *1*

INTRODUCTION

T. S. Eliot, like other poets, has suffered as much from his admirers as from his detractors. But the consequence for him has been an extraordinary ambiguity of opinion. As poet and critic he has been divided between novelty and tradition, both hailed and damned as exotic or academic. Indeed, these effects have not been exempt from confusion, for he has been thought to be at once too traditional and too novel, expressing trite matter in eccentric form. Thus we find judgment disconcerted, outside of politics and religion, by such illusive paradoxes as musical comedy in a Greek form or classicism in the garb of Ezra Pound. Too often we are reminded of Sweeney's words, "That don't apply." From the contrariety of his effects, the reader might be justified in concluding that his talent is alien to the English tradition.

The common reader, however, will be wiser to regard Eliot as a poet who makes demands upon his audience similar to those made by some older English poets, modified indeed by other influences and another age. To

place his poetry beside Browning's *Men and Women* is
to understand Ezra Pound's remark that "the form of
these poems is the most vital form of that period." The
questions we are moved to ask about his poetry are not
new; neither are the real answers. The novelty lies in
his manner of providing the answers. This presents a
difficulty that is often magnified because too much nov-
elty is assumed. It often takes shape upon the assump-
tion of what he omits, or of the kind of co-operation he
requires of his reader. It is often said, for example, that
he leaves out connections and transitions, but this is true
only in a grammatical sense. If he omits the grammatical
signs of connection and order, he preserves the psycho-
logical or poetic signs. No order, no discourse; but he
writes the discourse upon which all poetry depends. Be-
cause poetry has a higher kind of order than that of
prose it is not released from that order. Such a release
has been satirized by Wyndham Lewis:

> I sabotage the sentence! With me is the naked word . . .
> Return with me where I am crying with the gorilla and
>   the bird.

Certainly the question why one thing follows another
must still be answered in Eliot as in Donne, though the
answer be more implicit in one than in the other. Neither
an emotional nor a musical effect, if it is really such, can
be founded on incoherence.[1]

---

1. See Ezra Pound, *A B C of Reading* (1934), p. 139: "The value of
music as elucidation of verse comes from the attention it throws on to
the detail. Every popular song has at least one line or sentence that is
perfectly clear. This line fits the music. It has usually formed the music."

This study assumes that poetry as meaning is neither plain sense nor nonsense, but a form of imaginative sense. If we insist that a lyric poem does not *mean* but *is*, we assert not a different mode of being but that its emotional values cannot be translated. As plain sense its meaning becomes an abstraction; as imaginative sense it is always realizing something more than its obvious meaning, is always conveying a state of mind as well as ideas. Its sense is qualified rather than defined by emotion, but its emotion takes form in the figures and configuration which transmit its energy. Indeed, we can speak of the meaning of a poem as its mode of apprehension or as a synthetic principle controlling the elements in which its feelings take shape. On a lower level it is no more and no less than the metrical syntax of the poem. Without it a poem will function at random; without its consideration any discussion must be aimless, at best peripheral. Without it a poem cannot have an apprehensible being.

This means that in poetry the modes of intuition are made intelligible by the poem and become subject to inference. Though the subconscious has replaced "inspiration" in poetry, reason has not ceased both to manipulate and to receive its product. Any shaping assumes an intention which is ultimately realized as the significance of the form. Moreover, if poetry does not reveal intention, criticism is reduced to the uncontrolled response of impressionism. But poetry of the unconscious in any strict sense is a contradiction; otherwise the poet is a maker of accidents.

This book hopes to be of some use to the reader, not the critic, of T. S. Eliot. It is intended to question this not uncommon view of his poetry: above the verse forms, his poems present formal difficulties of a much more discouraging nature; often they seem not to make sense; sometimes they seem emotionally incoherent; now and then they sound even musically incoherent. The only recourse, if one is to read them, is to surrender oneself to the incantation without asking any questions, even when the spell is over; certainly not the questions that are answered by the older poets.

This book will no doubt suggest, with some pertinacity, that reading T. S. Eliot has a number of predicates denied by such a view. Not the least of these will be that reading his poetry is essentially like reading that of other poets; at most that he differs from other poets only as the intellectual element differentiates some poetry from that which is more direct or immediate in its emotional relation to life. In this relationship the light of his vision is refracted by more intellectual elements, but the poetic problems presented by this vision, as embodied in his verse, are not therefore of another kind from those usually presented by poetry. Though the more obvious signs of connection, for example, may be missing, the kinds of inference required are not of a different order. Poetry as the most highly ordered form of language involves some kind of syntax. If its principles of coherence are not merely those of prose, they do not negate those of prose. If these principles take particular forms in different poems, they still belong to some general category.

But, it may be objected, if reading Eliot is no different from reading other poets, why a book? It can be replied that, although the questions provoked by his poetry are not different, the answers are provided by less common means, which often require some elucidation. As Thomas Fuller might say, he sails to his goal by a side wind. Indirection and all forms of emotional reticence, notably those of irony, symbolic association, and antithetic metaphor (catachresis), occupy a much larger place in his poetry. Herein lies his novelty and the justification of a book. In the interest of lyric economy or functional intensity he is always concerned with what can be left out; or rather, what can be left implicit rather than made explicit. Although the connections are there, they are always performing some other function as well; they never merely connect. This other function frequently diverts attention from their connective function, which is commonly performed by an inference from, or an expectation created by, the preceding element. The connections are mental or psychological rather than verbal or grammatical. Similarly, the synthetic principle which integrates a group of particulars is frequently omitted; the principle of association, the general idea, must be inferred from the parts; the basic metaphor, to which the others relate, may be there but differentiated.

This economy increases the potential of each word and raises the significant intensity of their relationships.

Or it may be said, in words of *The Times Literary Supplement,* that his poetry has the "two marks of 'modernist' work, the liveliness that comes from topicality and the difficulty that comes from intellectual abstruseness." The topical and the intellectual, the lively and the difficult, these are superficial effects of modernist work; their reasons must be sought in the causes for such effects. In Eliot they derive from his fusion of the new and the old, interpreting one by the other, revealing the continuity of human experience, defining contemporaneity and tradition; they are integrated in his view of life. In the new and the old he finds both antithesis and similitude, often mingled in the paradox of the one and the many, or of time and the timeless. His acute perception of similarity and difference between the same things, his mixed use of the intellectual wits that Hobbes called fancy and judgment, is common in Metaphysical poetry or the poetic wit of the seventeenth century. This awareness produces the fusion which makes him both lively and difficult, at once novel and traditional. Informed by history or tradition, his sense of difference cooperates with his sense of likeness, and in his method finds satisfaction in forms that run from contrast to contrariety, or that point difference in likeness as well as likeness in difference, combining them in paradox or the metaphor of incompatibles by discovering a hidden congruity.

When Eliot objects to the practice in criticism of " 'interpretation' (I am not touching upon the acrostic element in literature)," [2] some critics may feel that in his parenthesis he has left an open door. The interest of the crossword puzzle is not absent from that of poetry; it is even recognized in Aristotle's discussion of metaphor; but it has one indispensable requirement, that the results not be trivial. On the interpretation of Eliot, however, some distinctions are certainly in order. To understand a poem in its own terms is not to interpret it; interpretation means translating it into other terms—to make "Prufrock" an allegory of modern man, or a document for psychoanalysis. What you get out of a poem must be found in it; a poem provides its own dictionary; you do not translate its terms by a dictionary to which no reference is made in the poem. If you choose to make "Prufrock" a personal testament or an allegory of modern man, that is your affair, but it is not the poem. "Comparison and analysis need only the cadavers on the table; but interpretation is always producing parts of the body from its pockets, and fixing them in place." [3] In psychoanalytic criticism, for example, the cadaver on the table is not the poem but the poet; in criticism it is necessary to identify the body that one is dissecting. When psychoanalysis translates imaginative symbols into psychic symbols and substitutes meanings defined by a science for those defined by a poem, it imposes

2. *Selected Essays,* p. 20.
3. *Ibid.,* p. 21.

upon the poem a system of metaphor at odds with its overt system. Even the allegorical reading of Eliot must correlate with the basic framework of the poem.

Neither does any particular belief constitute a poem. Beliefs may organize experience into meaning, but they do not determine poetic significance. The notion of the pre-existence of the soul may shape or even explain Wordsworth's "Intimations of Immortality," but it is neither the experience of early childhood nor the significance derived from it. Eliot's religious beliefs do not determine his poems any more than an allegory of modern man determines "Prufrock." His poems are not sermons, or substitutes for them, but at most the experience of religious feeling in our time. In good poets religious feeling has intensified rather than narrowed the sensibility and has deepened their awareness of life.

We need not become priests to the temple of Eliotese mysteries, or even intellectual snobs, in order to read him with appreciation. But he is not easy; nor does he compose riddles. As readers we need not give ourselves unnecessary handicaps—those insisted on by the Elect among his Understanders. For example, the need to discover every allusion. If awareness of an allusion is necessary, the poem will make it evident in some way. Dependence on notes for the recovery of learning is acceptable in reading poetry, but not dependence on notes for effects not realized in the poem. Here Eliot fails less than he is said to fail; indeed, his one venture into notes sometimes suggested effects other than those required

by the poem. Recovery of the allusions may enrich but
not replace the poet's meaning; it may also pervert it.
On the other hand, to condemn an Eliot poem on the
ground that it resembles a mosaic or pastiche of other
poems is to condemn no less a poem than Milton's
Lycidas. It is an old habit of poets, depending on mem-
ory's part in imagination, and if we are troubled by it we
should not read too widely.

In reading Eliot one is obliged to follow the order of
the ideas or the parts for the significance of their rela-
tionships. His suppression of ordinary connectives does
not mean either something esoteric or confusion and dis-
order. The succession of words is not random, but con-
nected or related—often in an obvious rather than a
devious way. Organizing principles are there, often
drawn from the commonest associational patterns. We
shall be failing the poem as well as the poet if we join
the disciples who are moved by the incantation without
understanding the words. It is of course a convenient
way of disowning uncongenial content or any obligation
to understand. But let us remember an elementary fact
too often ignored—that the medium of poetry is not pure
sound, but significant sounds with predetermined mean-
ings, which the poet may alter but never violate.

Eliot's oft-quoted statement that "genuine poetry can
communicate before it is understood" [4] is a doubtful
proposition relative to a foreign language; in a wider
sense it is truest of the poetry which provoked it,

4. *Selected Essays,* p. 200.

namely, the allegorical. But while Dante is making sense
on a veiled level, he is also making sense on an overt
level; his feeling is not undefined.

We may sympathize with those who argue that to ask
a poet what he is saying is to ask for an abstraction from
the poem. But the question is legitimate, even necessary.
For without some kind of answer we have no guide to
the experience and significance of the poem. Without
some notion of the larger and simpler aspect of the or-
ganization of the poem—its general progression—our
response to the subtler and more complex effects devel-
oped within it will not be intelligent. Without some idea
of its structural relations, the poem will have as much
ambiguity as Mr. Empson can discover. But no poet ever
contrived or explored ambiguities without thinking that
he was also controlling them; he did not think he was
writing a poetic dictionary, but a sentence. And the
poem is the sentence which limits the associations of its
words, limits the searcher for ambiguity.

When Mr. Cleanth Brooks denounces the heresy of
paraphrase, he means only that poetry has no synonyms,
that metaphor is not translatable, that a poem is an
experience rather than a meaning. But it is both—a
significant experience; and Brooks is always telling you
the meaning of poems, is always being a heretic. At
most he translates a poem into statements and its words
into meanings, collapsing the original structure into a
nest of metaphors or paradoxes. For the modish poetics
of our time explicit meaning is superseded by implicit

meanings because the mind or psyche is regarded at best as a factitious unity. Thus in poetry the welter of impulses finds order or unity only in a balance of tensions: order itself becomes a metaphor. Hence the real expression of a splintered mind is sought in irony or paradox or ambiguity.

But Aristotle, who held the power of finding similarity in difference supreme, was not absurd when he analyzed metaphor in the general terms of genus and species or analogy, and its translation of one into the other. In Hobbes the power of metaphor is called wit or fancy. Metaphors in poems are not relative without this more general meaning. For example, the field of meaning covered by "canonization" in Donne's poem, when related to secular love, enables Mr. Brooks, in *The Well-Wrought Urn,* to follow and to paraphrase Donne's poem. If he wished to avoid this heresy, he should merely have analyzed the poem into causes for its effects; instead, he gives his "reading" or translation of the poem, with some turns on sex that do not fit Donne's basic metaphor. Any meaning that is excluded by its primary context must be rejected. Hence an awareness of the principles of association or analogy by which the metaphors are organized, the syntax by which the terms are controlled, is necessary not only to an understanding of the poem but also to the reception of its full effect. In this sense we shall be concerned with significant structure, the implicit principles of organization and therefore meaning; and with the abstraction of these principles, with the translation of the concrete and particular into terms of the abstract and general. But all with a view to the fuller realization of the concrete and particular which is the poem.

Since poetry is a temporal art, a poem has both the limitations and the obligations of becoming. Where connections and transitions are left out, structure depends wholly upon the order of the parts. This order becomes the syntax of the poem. Within succession various kinds of order are possible, with appropriate forms of connection; such orders as temporal, incremental, logical, or psychological—from trains of association. Principles of coherence are discovered in the main figures of speech when reduced by Alexander Bain to three mental operations: the feeling of difference, the feeling of likeness or agreement, and the feeling of association. To ask why one part succeeds another is to ask the meaning of this order. If the poem is coherent (and even nonsense verse derives its effect from this assumption) the answer must be implicit, for a later part has its antecedent in an earlier part. The reference or connection may be made by such means as implication, affinity, natural consequence, similitude, or contrast. Here "post hoc, ergo propter hoc" (after this, therefore because of this) is a causal relation—not a fallacy.

And Eliot has sequential logic; that is, he employs rational connections, writes in accordance with the inferences which are probably to be drawn from certain situations, characters, actions, objects, responses, or relations. His "logic of imagery" does not mean incoherence but connection by a common principle or a series of probable associations; that is, associations which involve inference of some kind or belong to a pattern of experience. It means connecting by analogy, implicit relations, or a frame of allusion. When Brooks and Warren, in *Understanding Poetry*, keep saying of "Prufrock" that a figure or an allusion is "in character" they are appealing to a kind of logic, but they deny any rational connection to the poem. For them the poem has no structure; the character merely exposes himself, and in no particular order. Their phrase about "the structure of the flow of ideas"—itself a neat paradox—explains the nature of their commentary. It is less paradoxical that in the same poem I see a structure rather than a flow of ideas, for structure involves both distinction of parts and significant order.

It is to be hoped that this book will at least suggest the kind of questions to be asked in an Eliot poem; that if the answers which are offered should all prove wrong, the ways taken to those answers will not always prove blind alleys. No attempt has been made to give full readings or analyses of the poems; nor to recover all the borrowings or erudition of the poet; only to offer some guidance to the evident but not obvious pattern of the poems, at most to chart their course. The intention is not to try to state what a poem ultimately means, but what it is about, or the terms in which it is developed; at times merely to indicate the pivots on which the sense turns. If my treatment of symbols often seems too specific, the reader should remember the contrary vice of excessive vagueness. However distressing the results, I shall try neither to fake my awareness nor to evade elementary questions; if I seem to avoid difficulties, it may be presumed that I do not understand. For the reader of Eliot, or any other poet for that matter, there is no other basis of appreciation, and yet such candor is not easy to attain.

Chapter **2**

THE USE OF HIS CRITICISM

To the reader of Eliot's poetry his criticism offers instruction that cannot be ignored. For there we find concepts of poetry that tell us what to expect in the attitude, material, form, and method of the poet. It is no paradox that the poet as critic often tells us as much about himself as about the poet under observation. Hence we shall observe in Eliot the basic ideas that prepare the expectations of a reader of his poetry.

First of all, his criticism tells us that he is a conscious poet, who has speculated about the nature and function of poetry, particularly in our time. His poetry is the product of one who believes that poetry is neither play nor random experiment, nor something that is achieved without the fullest exertion of his powers. Nor is it, despite his vehement qualifications, something unrelated to experience, both his own and that of the race. The ease with which his theory of tradition for the poet passes into a theory of culture suggests the serious function that he assigns, however diffidently, to the use of poetry. This is to be remarked because he was once greeted as the writer of light society verse, but that view may now be taken as a sign of the unconventional aspect of his poetry.

Eliot is a poet of moral nature, or the history of man, not of physical nature or beauty or merely subjective life. His attitude has developed from the following position in *The Sacred Wood:*

> The contemplation of the horrid or sordid or disgusting, by an artist, is the necessary and negative aspect of the impulse toward the pursuit of beauty. But not all succeed as did Dante in expressing the complete scale from negative to positive. The negative is the more importunate. (p. 153)

For him this scale is magnified by time, and he views the contemporary scene with a full consciousness of the past, though he finds their difference more in consciousness than in time. Indeed, an acute awareness of the relations of present and past is central to his poetic sensitivity as well as his conception of human wisdom. This awareness, it need hardly be said, does not take form as the pathos of the flight of time; other relations of past and present form the central problem of his poetry. For him the problem of the future, ultimately the religious problem, can be resolved only in these terms. But the present, however repugnant, is never sacrificed either to the past or the future.

"Tradition and the Individual Talent" shows the importance, early and late, of the problem of time for

Eliot.[1] Essentially the same paradoxes reappear in *Four Quartets,* where they point the relation of temporal and spiritual things rather than the relation of contemporary talent to enduring tradition. As poet and as religious man his relation to the past, to time, has been the critical problem. His basic paradox has remained his dual relation to history, his sense of its pastness and its presence or of the changing and the permanent, toward the resolution of which his efforts have been constantly directed. It is the prime source of confusion in understanding him both as poet and as religious man; scrupulous honesty in recording his feelings toward both elements has bewildered those who have been concerned merely with one aspect, or have failed to recognize the other. While he seeks the permanent in the temporary, the timeless in time, he ultimately finds it on the religious level. He is the poet, in a deeper sense, of the historical consciousness. On whatever aspects the attention is directed from time to time, the problem is always the same, though the emotions brought into play are not. At first satiric or ironic, they run the gamut which he later describes as "the boredom, and the horror, and the glory."

When he regards the poet's mind as a medium rather than a personality, he insists on separating the man and the poet, experience and art; for man and experience

1. On the problem of time, especially in *Four Quartets,* see H. V. Routh, *English Literature and Ideas in the Twentieth Century,* pp. 143-45.

may exist without tradition, poet and art cannot. Ex-
perience enters into art, but it is thereby transformed
and loses its personal meaning in a more general mean-
ing. How this happens can only be learned from art,
its significance from history. At bottom impersonality
means that a poem is never mere self-expression, but
an experience which has an existence apart from the
poet; it is an ordering of experience which can recreate
itself in other minds, by means of what he calls the
"objective correlative." To this end he creates charac-
ters or employs the *persona* or mask, which may also
release images suppressed in himself. A poem is not a
personal letter from one individual to another, but a
composition in which the writer ceases to exist as such
and becomes the medium of an experience that belongs
to all who read and understand. "Shakespeare, too,"
says Eliot, "was occupied with the struggle—which
alone constitutes life for a poet—to transmute his per-
sonal and private agonies into something rich and
strange, something universal and impersonal." [2] The ex-
perience is generalized and stripped, as Rymer might
say, of its "accidental historical impudence." It is in
this sense that Eliot has asserted his classicism. Thus
in "Tradition and the Individual Talent" he attacks
"the metaphysical theory of the substantial unity of
the soul" to the extent of distinguishing sensibility from
personality in the poet. Later, in his epigraph, he sug-

---

2. *Selected Essays,* p. 117.

gests the region of escape from personality: "Mind is, no doubt, something more divine and impassible." In poetry the sensibility may divest itself of personality by attaining the region of impersonal significance.

In the same essay tradition is defined between the extremes of novelty and repetition; it means development; and it involves the historical sense:

> This historical sense, which is a sense of the timeless as well as of the temporal and of the timeless and of the temporal together, is what makes a writer traditional. And it is at the same time what makes a writer most acutely conscious of his place in time, of his own contemporaneity. (*Ibid.*, p. 4.)

Although art never improves, "the material of art is never quite the same." The poet must be aware that the collective mind "is a mind which changes, and that this change is a development which abandons nothing *en route*"; and he must learn that this mind is "much more important than his own private mind." Yet "the difference between the present and the past is that the conscious present is an awareness of the past in a way and to an extent which the past's awareness of itself cannot show." [3] The full meaning of this on the spiritual level is explored in *Four Quartets*. Now Eliot concludes: "What is to be insisted upon is that the poet must develop or procure the consciousness of the past and that he should continue to develop this consciousness throughout his career." Ultimately this awareness of the past—later developed in a new way—is what makes

---

3. *Selected Essays,* p. 6.

the poet acutely conscious of the present. Then, with the aid of the famous catalyst analogy, he defines the process of depersonalization for the poet, which is related to the sense of tradition. Thus he defines the relation of poetry both to the mind of the past and to his own private mind; in subordinating the latter to the former he is subordinating the temporal to the permanent.

Granted poetic sensibility, the poet in his theory intensifies his sensibility and widens his vision by an awareness of history. For history makes or keeps him aware of the larger significance or relationship of his feelings. In Eliot's poetry what appear to be merely contrasts of present and past, often by literary quotation or allusion, are consequences of this view of history, this sense of tradition or permanent human values. Though a work of art is impersonal, it presents a view of life: "Marlowe's and Jonson's comedies were a view of life; they were, as great literature is, the transformation of a personality into a personal work of art, their lifetime's work, long or short." [4] Although the poet's mind is a medium and its product impersonal, both depend upon experience; and this whole complex of ideas for Eliot depends upon Remy de Gourmont's conception of the artist as transferring or translating himself drop by drop into his works, outside of which he is of little interest. But the artist needs something to translate, and he can fail, as Eliot finds Massinger

4. *Ibid.*, p. 192.

failing, because of a defect of personality: "He is not, however, the only man of letters who, at the moment when a new view of life is wanted, has looked at life through the eyes of his predecessors, and only at manners through his own." [5] He was "killed by conventions which were suitable for the preceding literary generation"; he failed to develop tradition, to renew it by his own talent or sensibility.

When Eliot finds the alliance of levity and seriousness a characteristic of wit and "a quality of a sophisticated literature," he remarks:

When we come to Gray and Collins, the sophistication remains only in the language, and has disappeared from the feeling. Gray and Collins were masters, but they had lost that hold on human values, that firm grasp of human experience, which is a formidable achievement of the Elizabethan and Jacobean poets. This wisdom, cynical perhaps but untired (in Shakespeare, a terrifying clairvoyance), leads toward, and is only completed by, the religious comprehension; it leads to the point of the *Ainsi tout leur a craqué dans la main* of Bouvard and Pecuchet. (*Ibid.*, p. 256.)

In 1921 these were prophetic words indeed for his own poetry; but also indicative of his requirements for poetry, particularly in its hold on human values, for which his sense of tradition is necessary. Thus literature not only depends upon personal experience, but in its representation exhibits, at its best, a hold on human values that finally determines its quality.

The famous catalyst analogy, which serves to de-

5. *Ibid.*, p. 195.

velop the idea of the poetic mind as a medium, directs
our attention to the kinds of material involved. They
are two, emotions and feelings. Feelings are not the
primary emotions of human nature, but more tenuous
and indefinite feelings "inhering for the writer in par-
ticular words or phrases or images." As man he experi-
ences the common emotions; as poet he develops them
by means of feelings that are not products of imme-
diate experience but rather of induced connections of
experience. It is not the given emotion but the unex-
pected contexts or associations that create the "new
art emotion." One consequence of this theory he has
observed relative to a borrowing in Marlowe—that his
"talent, like that of most poets, was partly synthetic." [6]
If the business of the poet is to use the ordinary emo-
tions "and, in working them up into poetry, to express
feelings which are not in actual emotions at all," [7] it
is to be done by associating with the basic or struc-
tural emotion a number of floating feelings which will
transmute or transform it into a new art emotion. The
materials lead Eliot to regard the poet's mind as "a
receptacle for seizing and storing up numberless feel-
ings, phrases, images, which remain there until all the
particles which can unite to form a new compound are
present together." [8] In the mind of the poet these feel-
ings are constantly forming new wholes, but of their

6. *Ibid.*, p. 102.
7. *Ibid.*, p. 10.
8. *Ibid.*, p. 8. Cf. *The Use of Poetry*, pp. 140-41.

character and their union something more is to be said. For poverty in them explains the lack of sophistication in Gray and Collins.

The poetic mind as a medium depends upon a unified sensibility, and this is simply a habit of mind which does not separate its experiences or responses, but cultivates their real or potential interactions. In expression this synthetic mind neither dissociates its powers nor sorts its reactions; it projects rather than analyzes its experience. Hence the "objective correlative":

> The only way of expressing emotion in the form of art is by finding an "objective correlative"; in other words, a set of objects, a situation, a chain of events which shall be the formula of that *particular* emotion; such that when the external facts, which must terminate in sensory experience, are given, the emotion is immediately evoked. (*Ibid.*, pp. 124-25.)

It is also the means "of transmuting ideas into sensations, of transforming an observation into a state of mind." [9] That "particular emotion," it will be remembered, is distinguished from similar emotions by its association with or qualification by conjoined feelings. In this correlative function the objects become symbols or acquire meanings beyond their usual ones. Where Coleridge calls this synthetic power imagination, Eliot speaks of it as a mechanism of sensibility.

The qualities of its product, however, derive in part from the nature of the materials amalgamated. In his

---

9. *Ibid.*, p. 249

famous Spinoza—cooking example [10] his emphasis is on "amalgamating disparate experience"; and from this fusion various effects of wit or surprise derive. But in speaking of the process [11] it is "the intensity of the artistic process, the pressure, so to speak, under which the fusion takes place, that counts." Their union is found less by imaginative insight into the objects themselves than by their association with related feelings in the poet; their union is established not by the intensity of the feelings themselves but by the emotional compulsion which brings them together, by the degree to which one feeling modifies another. He illustrates this union by the way in which the nightingale brings a number of feelings together in the ode of Keats. Of course this union or form involves order for its significance: "the ordinary man's experience is chaotic, irregular, fragmentary"; [12] in the poet's mind disparate experiences are always forming new wholes. And the union of disparates is the basis of wit in poetry, whether they are "tough reasonableness" and "slight lyric grace," "levity" and "seriousness," or other disparate qualities.[13] For upon such contrasts depends the element of surprise which constitutes poetic wit. In Donne it derives from "rapid alterations and antitheses" of feeling.

10. *Ibid.*, p. 247.
11. *Ibid.*, p. 8.
12. *Ibid.*, p. 247.
13. *Ibid.*, p. 252. For example, Gray and Collins, "with all their accredited purity, are comparatively poor in shades of feeling to contrast and unite" (p. 261).

It is noteworthy that in elucidating poetic wit Eliot [14] quotes Coleridge on the imagination to show how wit passes into its operation. Because of his own emphasis on sensibility "every vital development in language is a development of feeling as well." [15] Massinger's verse is deficient because, though different from that of his predecessors, "it is not a development based on, or resulting from, a new way of feeling." [16] An involved style "should follow the involutions of a mode of perceiving, registering, and digesting impressions which is also involved." [17] For his unified sensibility, which is the medium of personality in the poet,

> One of the surest of tests is the way in which a poet borrows. Immature poets imitate; mature poets steal; bad poets deface what they take, and good poets make it into something better, or at least something different. The good poet welds his theft into a whole of feeling which is unique, utterly different from that from which it was torn; the bad poet throws it into something which has no cohesion. A good poet will usually borrow from authors remote in time, or alien in language, or diverse in interest. (*Ibid.*, p. 182.)

The whole of feeling into which the good poet welds his theft shows how the emotional pressure of the artistic process dominates its materials. For tradition this use of other poets is intended not to preserve their meaning but to make it contemporary.

---

14. *Ibid.*, p. 256.
15. *Ibid.*, p. 185.
16. *Ibid.*, p. 186. See *The Sacred Wood* (p. 57): "To create a form is not merely to invent a shape, a rhyme or rhythm. It is also the realization of the whole appropriate content of this rhyme or rhythm."
17. *Ibid.*, p. 187.

The main consequences of this theory for his own poetry will become evident to the reader, but one of the results may be suggested. His lyric themes generally are complex, requiring complicated procedures. These are often dramatic in nature, employing the impersonal projection indicated by his theory, but treating not so much conflict in action as in thought and emotion, where antithesis, paradox, incompatible metaphor, irony, and other forms of discord or discordant concord become the proper means of expression. Often his expression depends upon the association, not resemblance, of ideas; then it works by the suggestion of metonyms or antonyms or other related terms, and connects by some affinity or implication.

Eliot's introduction to *Ezra Pound: Selected Poems* in 1928 applies or develops some of these earlier doctrines. His definition of originality, for instance, derives from his ideas of tradition and the individual talent. True originality is merely development of the art of one's predecessors, and genuine when a logical development. It is a shallow test of originality to say that the original poet goes direct to life, and the derivative poet to literature; for the derivative poet in fact mistakes literature for life. We should not "confuse the material and the use which the author makes of it." We should understand that "if one can really penetrate the life of another age, one is penetrating the life of one's own." When Pound sees Provence and medieval Italy as contemporary with himself, "he has grasped

certain things in Provence and Italy which are perma-
nent in human nature. He is much more modern, in
my opinion, when he deals with Italy and Provence,
than when he deals with modern life."

In its various assimilations the work of Pound re-
veals "a steady effort towards the synthetic construc-
tion of a style of speech." But technical accomplishment
and deeper personal feeling are not always found
united, for the two are not always simultaneous in their
development.

The poet's progress is dual. There is the gradual accumu-
lation of experience, like a tantalus jar: it may be only once
in five or ten years that experience accumulates to form a
new whole and finds its appropriate expression. But if a poet
were content to attempt nothing less than always his best, if
he insisted on waiting for these unpredictable crystalliza-
tions, he would not be ready for them when they came. The
development of experience is largely unconscious, subter-
ranean, so that we cannot gauge its progress except once in
every five or ten years; but in the meantime the poet must be
working; he must be experimenting and trying his technique
so that it will be ready, like a well-oiled fire-engine, when
the moment comes to strain it to its utmost. (p. xviii.)

This passage presents the other aspect of the catalyst
theory, the mind as receptacle. While poetry attends
upon the accumulation of experience, which develops
subconsciously, the mind as a unified sensibility is still
the medium of transmutation. Then Eliot explains the
masterpiece in these terms:

. . . a poet's work may proceed along two lines on an imagi-
nary graph; one of the lines being his conscious and con-

tinuous effort in technical excellence, that is, in continually developing his medium for the moment when he really has something to say. The other line is just his normal human course of development, his accumulation and digestion of experience (experience is not sought for, it is merely accepted in consequence of doing what we really want to do), and by experience I mean the results of reading and reflection, varied interests of all sorts, contacts and acquaintances, as well as passion and adventure. Now and then the two lines may converge at a high peak, so that we get a masterpiece. That is to say, an accumulation of experience has crystallized to form material of art, and years of work in technique have prepared an adequate medium; and something results in which medium and material, form and content, are indistinguishable. (p. xx.)

This coincidence gives perfection of form united with significance of feeling. Pound once induced him to destroy what he thought an excellent set of couplets, because Pope had done it better. His couplets were not a development based on a new way of feeling.

When Pound insists on "an element of humour, of irony and mockery, in Propertius," Eliot's conclusion that "Propertius was more civilized than most of his interpreters have admitted" is significant; he made a similar requirement in his essay on Marvell. Humour, irony, mockery, wit, all are signs of civilization for him and hence of superior poetry. But there are other signs of such poetry:

I know very well that the apparent roughness and *naiveté* of the verse and rhyming of *Mauberley* are inevitably the result of many years of hard work: if you cannot appreciate the dexterity of *Altaforte* you cannot appreciate the simplicity of *Mauberley*. On the other side, the poem seems to me, when you have marked the sophistication and the great variety of the verse, verse of a man who knows his way about, to be a positive document of sensibility. It is compact of the experience of a certain man in a certain place at a certain time; and it is also a document of an epoch; it is genuine tragedy and comedy; and it is, in the best sense of Arnold's worn phrase, a "criticism of life." (p. xxiv.)

Here Eliot's two lines come together, with appropriate emphasis on sensibility, but even more upon the translation of individual experience into the general significance of art.

His introduction to St.-J. Perse, though directed to the reader of *Anabase*, contains the most particular suggestions for reading his own poetry. Their relevance, which is a relevance to his own school of poetry, is immediately obvious. Eliot did not have to borrow this explanation of *Anabasis*, or of his own poems:

. . . that any obscurity of the poem, on first readings, is due to the suppression of "links in the chain," or explanatory and connecting matter, and not to incoherence, or to the love of cryptogram. The justification of such abbreviation of method is that the sequence of images coincides and concentrates into one intense impression of barbaric civilization. The reader has to allow the images to fall into his memory successively without questioning the reasonableness of each at the moment; so that, at the end, a total effect is produced.

This posits both an end and reasonableness in the method; it might be offered as an explanation of *The Waste Land*. Then he proceeds to defend this method:

Such selection of a sequence of images and ideas has nothing chaotic about it. There is a logic of the imagination as well as a logic of concepts. People who do not appreciate poetry always find it difficult to distinguish between order and chaos in the arrangement of images; and even those who are capable of appreciating poetry cannot depend upon first impressions.

He suggests that "such an arrangement of imagery requires just as much 'fundamental brain-work' as the arrangement of an argument," and thus reminds us that the modern Symbolist, unlike the Metaphysical poet, avoids overt logic even more than overt metaphor. But if we regard Symbolist poems as metaphors in which the major terms are not named, Eliot is not a Symbolist. Indeed, he has leaned to the conclusion that "the suggestiveness of true poetry . . . is the aura around a bright clear centre, that you cannot have the aura alone." [18]

On the subject of verse he also gives us some insight into his own practice:

It would be convenient if poetry were always verse—either accented, alliterative, or quantitative; but that is not true. Poetry may occur, within a definite limit on one side, at any point along a line of which the formal limits are "verse" and "prose."

By using "certain exclusively poetic methods" it is possible "to write poetry in what is called prose." Though *Anabase* approaches prose, it is poetry:

18. *Selected Essays*, p. 259.

Its sequences, its logic of imagery, are those of poetry and not of prose; and in consequence—at least the two methods are very closely allied—the *declamation,* the system of stresses and pauses, which is partially exhibited by the punctuation and spacing, is that of poetry and not of prose.

While its basic pattern resembles the serried phrasing of Biblical declamation, *Anabase* also suggests the alexandrine, and is free verse in the sense in which Eliot understands *vers libre,* not as an escape, but as a development. He defines the term in his introduction to Pound:

> The *vers libre* of Jules Laforgue, who, if not quite the greatest French poet after Baudelaire, was certainly the most important technical innovator, is free verse in much the way that the later verse of Shakespeare, Webster, Tourneur, is free verse: that is to say, it stretches, contracts, and distorts the traditional French measure as later Elizabethan and Jacobean poetry stretches, contracts and distorts the blank verse measure. (p. viii.)

And then he relates it to his own verse:

> My own verse is, so far as I can judge, nearer to the original meaning of *vers libre* than is any of the other types: at least, the form in which I began to write, in 1908 or 1909, was directly drawn from the study of Laforgue together with the later Elizabethan drama; and I do not know anyone who started from exactly that point.

In his extension of a traditional measure, chiefly by keeping stress equivalence and developing phrasal modulation, Eliot illustrates the proper relation of "tradition and the individual talent." Possibly he renewed his verse by the phrasal system encountered in his translation of *Anabase;* at all events, one may look at the *Choruses from "The Rock"* in that light. One may learn from all this to look at Eliot's verse in relation to traditional measures before one calls it merely free, and to look for an implicit order in his poems before one calls them chaotic.

Eliot's progress in verse might be outlined as follows: from loose verse forms with a blank verse basis, variously sectioned, and functionally rhymed; or accented forms in shorter lines; to regular stanza forms, with an occasional irregular element, curt in movement, zoned and emphasized by rhyme; to stretched or syncopated modulations of earlier forms, more variously rhythmed —more accentual than syllabic in metre, like nursery rhymes or the *Samson Agonistes* chorus—eschewing punctuation or replacing it by verse divisions, introducing punctuation only where verse pauses do not suffice. In the stanzas the formal pattern may be further formalized by grouping them into antithetic or contrasting parts. In *Sweeney Agonistes* the accentual balance of metre and rhetoric is modified by a sharper inflection of the phrase. The later verse—begun in the Ariel poems —is varied between lax and taut rhythms of different lengths, or between free and regular forms.

In his essay on Marlowe, Eliot made significant observations:

Marlowe gets into blank verse the melody of Spenser, and he gets a new driving power by reinforcing the sentence period against the line period . . . Marlowe went further: he broke up the line, to a gain in intensity . . . and he developed a new and important conversational tone. (*Selected Essays*, p. 104.)

These are effects that Eliot too has sought. In declamation he moves from a free dramatic blank verse to a freer manipulation of his accentual base, molded by phrasal modulation on fewer stresses, more indulgent to longer and looser rhythms of similar shape, more accommodated to speech. Throughout, his arrangement of words by line, his spacing, must be carefully regarded not only for the musical phrases and pauses, but also for their relation to the logical sequence which, by crossing the line division, points the significance of their disposition. Where the syntax of the paragraph seems to be floating—where verse displaces punctuation—a few readings will usually reveal the units that belong together. Modulation or change in the verse form introduces various kinds of change or transition in the subject or feeling; it often does the work of the more common forms of transition. To understand the beauty of Eliot's verse one may listen to the records that have been made of his readings.

But Eliot has sometimes given comfort to those who find his poetry chaotic. While explaining the failure of *Kubla Khan*,[19] he argues that its imagery is not used, not organized significantly. He contends that imagery in poetry must be "used," that "even the finest line draws its life from its context"; but then he adds that

19. *The Use of Poetry*, pp. 139-40.

the organization of all good poetry does not reach quite to the level of a "rational use and justification" of its imagery. And he proceeds to suggest that in this event the imagery derives its intensity from its saturation "with feelings too obscure for the authors even to know quite what they were." After illustrating various memories, he adds that "such memories may have symbolic value, but of what we cannot tell, for they come to represent the depths of feeling into which we cannot peer." While this is no doubt true of their "personal saturation value," it is equally true that in poems we must be able to peer into them if they are used as symbols; if they do not become symbols, their value will be nonexistent for us, since it is essentially private.

Although a memory is a private affair, why or at least how it comes at a certain juncture is a concern of the poem and therefore of the reader. Indeed, among the memories cited by Eliot, there is one that allows us to see how it became a public affair in the *Journey of the Magi*. But if an image is "used" in his sense, it is no longer dependent upon its private associations, and something can be said about its use. Since Eliot declares that "organization is necessary as well as 'inspiration,' " the seventeenth century Whichcote may add the alternative, "If you say you have a revelation from God, I must have a revelation from God too before I can believe you."

Eliot himself has raised the problem of meaning in

a poem. In *The Use of Poetry and the Use of Criticism* he declares:

> The chief use of the "meaning" of a poem, in the ordinary sense, may be (for here again I am speaking of some kinds of poetry and not all) to satisfy one habit of the reader, to keep his mind diverted and quiet, while the poem does its work upon him: much as the imaginary burglar is always provided with a bit of nice meat for the house-dog. (p. 144.)

While this is a normal situation of which he approves, he adds that the minds of all poets do not work that way. But he is not to be numbered among those who "become impatient of this 'meaning' which seems superfluous, and perceive possibilities of intensity through its elimination." Later, in his introduction to G. Wilson Knight's *Wheel of Fire*, he remarks: "Now it is only a personal prejudice of mine, that I prefer poetry with a clear philosophical pattern, if it has the other pattern as well, to poetry like Shakespeare's." The other pattern is an implicit or symbolic meaning, not the "systematic pattern." Philosophical pattern of course admits even more of meaning in the ordinary sense into poetry. And by separating the symbolic pattern Eliot now recognizes the human impulse to "interpret," but he limits its solid results to those which can be agreed on by qualified judges—in short, to some kind of ascertainable meaning. Of course this testifies to the strength of another habit of the reader.

Yet Eliot may seem to encourage the elimination of meaning when he remarks that "the poem may begin to shape itself in fragments of musical rhythm, and its structure will first appear in terms of something analogous to musical form." But if, as he says, "the music of verse is inseparable from the meanings and associations of words," then the meanings are no less terms of ordering and organizing poems, and a means of greater precision—at least, more articulate—than either music or associations. In fact, these qualities of words provide different aspects or kinds of context by which poems are organized; but the initial stage of their organization is not equivalent to their completed form. His most comprehensive statement on rhythm and meaning is found in *The Music of Poetry.*

We shall be concerned with the more overt pattern of meaning in the poem, not with "interpretation"; with what he calls the plane of order, not of pattern. The scheme of meaning, which supports the poetic structure, limits and controls the range of response to the poem. It is implied in the " 'objective correlative'; in other words, a set of objects, a situation, a chain of events which shall be the formula of that *particular* emotion." Thus meaning makes the emotion particular, for this framework places the feeling by means of a context. The consideration of a poem's meaning or framework involves an examination of its fundamental relations and its allusive materials—its intentional associations. And the scheme of its meaning is necessary to an understanding and judgment of the emotional structure of the poem, since that structure derives from the formula of the objective correlative. Unless the reader knows what the poem is about, he is moved, if he is moved at all, to no purpose. Without such perception, there can be no significant feeling. With such perception, multiple readings are not only illegitimate but impossible, except within fixed limits. If poems surrender their personal and private meaning for the author only to acquire a personal and private meaning for the reader, there is no sense in their claim to the universal and impersonal character of art. And there is little sense in our discussing a poem which exists in as many different forms as it has readers.

Chapter 3

PRUFROCK AND
OTHER OBSERVATIONS

The title of Eliot's first volume, which provides the heading for this chapter, immediately suggests the observer and an objective attitude. Nevertheless, these observations are made to convey feelings rather than novel perceptions of the social scene. They are—certainly the chief titles—Laforgian poems; for Laforgue has inspired Eliot in method and verse, not to say mood. The influence is as much in the emotional attitude as in the technique of verse. The Laforgian method, moreover, is the instrument of a mood that connects it, for Eliot, with the seventeenth century Metaphysical poets. This method may be summarized as the assumption of an ironic mask or attitude, mock-heroic in effect and wit, expressing a mixed mood, often by dramatic means. It indulges in self-mockery or ridicules serious feeling; it represents mixed reactions to things, the subjective mocked by the objective, the discrepancy between appearance and reality. It sees boredom and horror, the frustration or derision of latent feeling, the shams of modern life; it dissimulates sympathy for their victims.

But this irony is also the reticence of a sensitive man, and satire its revenge. It would be possible to treat his changing method, which emerges from the *personae* or attitudes objectified in his poems, as an evolution or attainment of greater and greater psychological directness. As he himself has said, while urging the impersonal character of poetry, "But, of course, only those who have personality and emotions know what it means to want to escape from these things." In basic method, however, he begins with the dramatic monologue or dialogue which unites Donne, Browning, Laforgue, and Corbière in his essay on *Donne in Our Time*. But for Eliot, too, this pattern remains more lyric than dramatic, less objective than subjective: "and with Donne and the French poets, the pattern is given by what goes on within the mind, rather than by the exterior events which provoke the mental activity and play of thought and feeling."

On the relation of modern or Laforgian poetry to Metaphysical poetry Eliot has been explicit. His essay on the Metaphysical poets closes on this note. Of the affinity which he observes we should take some notice. The reason we get "a method curiously similar to that of the 'metaphysical poets' " is provided by this passage:

Our civilization comprehends great variety and complexity, and this variety and complexity, playing upon a refined sensibility, must produce various and complex results. The poet must become more and more comprehensive, more al-

lusive, more indirect, in order to force, to dislocate if neces-
sary, language into his meaning.[1]

Laforgue and Corbière are named as being "nearer to
the school of Donne than any modern English poet,"
having "the same essential quality"—found also in
Baudelaire—"of transmuting ideas into sensations, of
transforming an observation into a state of mind." This
achievement should be kept in mind while reading
Eliot's observations.

To this method his definition of wit in the essay on
Marvell is also relevant. After calling it "a tough reason-
ableness beneath the slight lyric grace," or "this alliance
of levity and seriousness (by which the seriousness is
intensified)," he clarifies what he means by "toughness":

> It [wit] is not cynicism, though it has a kind of toughness
> which may be confused with cynicism by the tender-minded.
> It is confused with erudition because it belongs to an edu-
> cated mind, rich in generations of experience; and it is con-
> fused with cynicism because it implies a constant inspection
> and criticism of experience.[2]

This definition may be related to the mood and method
which have been ascribed to Laforgue; in both the
Laforgian and Metaphysical poet levity intensifies seri-
ousness. Wit also has its relation to "Tradition and the
Individual Talent," and it is further qualified by this
observation:

---

1. *Selected Essays*, p. 248.
2. *Ibid.*, p. 262.

And nowadays we find occasionally good irony, or satire, which lack wit's internal equilibrium, because their voices are essentially protests against some outside sentimentality or stupidity; or we find serious poets who seem afraid of acquiring wit, lest they lose intensity.[3]

This wit is a manifestation of that sense of tradition which he urges the poet to acquire. It is the sense of fact which he insists on in "The Function of Criticism" applied to experience; it goes with the classical mind of that essay, and was once expressed by Eliot in these words:

The romantic is deficient or undeveloped in his ability to distinguish between fact and fancy, whereas the classicist, or adult mind, is thoroughly realist—without illusions, without day-dreams, without hope, without bitterness, and with an abundant resignation.

In the Marvell essay it is the "recognition, implicit in the expression of every experience, of other kinds of experience which are possible."

These elements in Eliot are better understood in terms of his background. His literary background is perhaps best summarized by the three periods of "metaphysical" poetry which he has distinguished: Medieval: school of Cavalcanti or Dante; Renaissance: school of Donne; Modern: school of Baudelaire or Laforgue.[4] He is sufficient witness on his indebtedness to the first two, but Ezra Pound has best described his relation to the third. Pound has remarked that Laforgue taught the

---

3. *Ibid.*, p. 263.
4. This information derives from reports of his Clark Lectures, which were never published.

early Eliot a "subtle conversational tone"; an elegant,
even dandified, irony—which connects with Baudelaire;
taught him how to construct an "ironic summary" of his
time, and in the process to convey himself. Pound ap-
plies Remy de Gourmont's phrase to both: "he recounts
himself in recounting the manners of his age." [5]

Pound regards the talent of Laforgue as that of "deli-
cate irony, the citadel of the intelligent"; he describes
his manner of using it in these words: "He deals for the
most part with literary poses and clichés, yet he makes
them a vehicle for the expression of his own very per-
sonal emotion, of his own unperturbed sincerity." To
this end he is a master of good verbalism, of conscious
cliché, of the international tongue of the excessively cul-
tivated; and he knows how to point scientific terminol-
ogy. To many people, says Pound, "why such powei
should coincide with so great a nonchalance of manner,
will remain forever a mystery." [6] More than one critic
of Eliot has made similar remarks without mentioning
Laforgue. Much later, in *The Criterion* (XII, 469), Eliot
himself gives another definition of this irony—especially
as found in "Prufrock"—when he observes its "use (as by
Jules Laforgue) to express a *dédoublement* of the per-
sonality against which the subject struggles."

But the problem of the early Eliot, which is the prob-
lem of Laforgue posed by Pound, is partly explained by
Eliot's "metaphysical" inheritance. The power of Mar⸱

5. See "Eliot" in *Instigations* (1920).
6. See "Laforgue" in *Instigations*.

vell, although defined by Eliot out of Coleridge, has
been learned from Laforgue and the Metaphysicals,
particularly how to juxtapose and fuse the opposite or
discordant, how to fuse emotion and wit. Indeed, few
Metaphysical preachers, as Eliot knows, could forget
that emotion and witty paradox met in the Nativity,
when "the Word was made flesh." Lancelot Andrewes
exclaimed, "What, *Verbum infans,* the Word an infant?
The Word, and not be able to speak a word?" And this
was also the great fusion of the ideal and the real. For
the Metaphysicals abstractions took on the "superficies"
of sense, but for them the superficies of sense were often
less vivid than abstractions. If Eliot has included Caval-
canti among the Metaphysicals, Pound was perhaps the
first to contrast the "interpretive metaphor" of Caval-
canti with the "ornamental metaphor" of Petrarch.[7]

On the subject of imitation Eliot has a remark to
which improper attention has been paid. In *The Use of
Poetry and the Use of Criticism* (p. 46) he speaks of
Ben Jonson's requisites for the poet, of which the first
two are talent and practice: "His third requisite in a
poet pleases me especially: 'The third requisite in our
poet, or maker, is *Imitation,* to be able to convert the
substance, or riches of another poet, to his own use.'"
Too often in Eliot the substance is marked and the
conversion ignored, but it is fatal for the reader not to
observe it. Let the reader be on guard for this conver-
sion in his use of the manner or attitude as well as

---

7. See *Make It New,* p. 361.

substance of another poet. There can be little doubt
that his adoption of the Laforgue manner brought to
fruition the experience of his earlier years, and we can
mark similar means in both, but we shall do well not
to equate either the experience or emotion found in
each. For an insight into these we shall be on safer
ground if we scrutinize his chapter on Arnold in *The
Use of Poetry,* and particularly the passage in which he
rebukes Arnold for his attitude toward Burns: "But the
essential advantage for a poet is not to have a beautiful
world with which to deal: it is to be able to see beneath
both beauty and ugliness; to see the boredom, and the
horror, and the glory." From the first Eliot enjoyed,
though in less degree, this advantage; and there is no
passage in his work that comes nearer to characterizing
his vision. His poetry is eloquent of his vision of the
boredom and the horror; but his vision of the glory has
been more imperfectly and painfully achieved. Yet it
has the integrity which comes from not ignoring the
others.

The Love Song of J. Alfred Prufrock

The mixture of levity and seriousness immediately
confronts the reader in the title poem of his first volume.
For he transposes his epigraph from the serious context
of Dante's *Inferno* to the lighter context of Prufrock's
love song. The epigraph is never to be ignored in Eliot;
for while it is not an essential part of the poem, it con-

veys hints of the significance or even genesis of the
poem. Together with the title, it prepares the reader
for the experience of the poem. Thus the first rule in
reading one of Eliot's poems is to consider the possibili-
ties suggested by the title and epigraph.

In this poem (1915) we have the love song of a cer-
tain character, whose very name is suggestive of quali-
ties he subsequently manifests.[8] Then the epigraph
states the situation of another character, who was called
upon to reveal himself. How is it related to the title?
Are the two characters alike or merely in similar situa-
tions? In view of the disparity which we have already
noted, let us proceed on the assumption that likeness in
situation is more likely to explain the presence of the
epigraph. What, then, is the situation? In the *Inferno*
(xxvii, 61–66) the flame of Guido is asked to identify
himself—"so may thy name on earth maintain its front"
—and he replies, in the words of the epigraph: "If I
thought my answer were to one who ever could return
to the world, this flame should shake no more; but since
none ever did return alive from this depth, if what I
hear be true, without fear of infamy I answer thee."
Obviously, if this relates to Prufrock, it must be an
extended metaphor which will gradually unfold itself.[9]

---

8. If Eliot's proper names do not acquire meaning from history or
literature or etymology, they are used for their generic or social sug-
gestion.

9. My exposition is indebted to the analysis by Roberta Morgan and
Albert Wohlstetter in *The Harvard Advocate* for December 1938. But
see *The Criterion* "Commentary" for April 1933 on Laforgue's use of
irony to express a division or doubling of the personality.

The first line of the poem introduces a "you and I" at a point in a debate at which the subjective "I" is surrendering to the more objective "you" and agreeing to go somewhere. Who are the "you and I" and where are they going? The "I" is the speaker, but who is the "you" addressed? The title would suggest a lady, but the epigraph suggests a scene out of the world, on a submerged level. Is the "I" giving in to a lady? Going to a more acceptable rendezvous? Or is he submitting for the moment to an urgent "you," with whom he is not in harmony?

It is evening, tea-time as we shall see. But the evening has an unusual character; as something seen through the eyes of the speaker, it derives its character from the speaker. This speaker is, we know, submissive —if we cannot say reluctant. Now he sees the evening in the aspect of etherization, and the metaphor of etherization suggests the desire for inactivity to the point of enforced release from pain. All of this simply projects the mind of the speaker—a mind, it would appear, that is in conflict, but presumably concerned with love.

After we learn the time of the going, colored by the speaker's mind, we learn the way of the going; and, considering the suggested character, it is a surprising way, through a cheap section of town. But it further characterizes the argument, tedious but insidious because leading to an "overwhelming question." The streets suggest the character of the question at their end as well as the nature of the urge which takes this route. The abrupt break after the mention of the question suggests an emotional block, which is emphasized by the refusal to identify the question. The urge seems to belong to the "you" and the block to the "I". Yet we are given an object of going in "our visit," though the real purpose has been evaded. This closes the first section and is followed by a stanzaic pause.

The most obvious question that "visit" provokes is "where" and this is answered by "in the room." But it is more than answered; it is qualified, again by the speaker's mind: his destination is a room in which women talk of the sculptor of heroic figures—no doubt trivial talk, but none the less of Michelangelo. After this recall of his destination, he turns back to the immediate scene —immediate at least in his psychological drama, or interior monologue.

With the image of the fog as cat we have another reflection of his mental state: desire which ends in inertia. If the cat image suggests sex, it also suggests the greater desire of inactivity. The speaker sees the evening in aspects of somnolence, or of action lapsing into inaction, both artificial and natural—sleep and etherization. The fog's settling down prompts the reflection that "indeed there will be time" for its more suggestive activity, and for his own. It may be observed that Eliot also follows Ben Jonson's rule for disposition: that each part provide the "cue" to the following part. "Time" now associates the scene with his mental indecision, but time also offers him an escape. This escape is good, however, only until the crucial moment for the question arrives; and it will be observed how the tension mounts as the time shortens, reaching a climax when he must "begin."

As he takes comfort in postponement, in the future, he amplifies the contemplated action in its "overwhelming" aspect with a violence of similitude that began with the metaphor of etherization. This also adds to the growing tension. And this violence of similitude is functional: it expresses emotions or states of mind; its exaggeration often explodes into gentle ridicule, provides the excess by which excessive feeling is perceived and measured. But there will be time for what? To prepare a face for the ordeal? Or rather "to meet the faces that you meet"? His self-conscious accommodation to the social scene suggests the same thing in others. This action is given an incongruous violence by the phrase "to murder and create"—relative to one face or being and another. The same kind of mock-heroic contrast appears in the un-Hesiodic "works and days of hands," though it also magnifies the "question." And there will be time for the two of them, you and me, at least before the event. This section ends by making precise the moment for the "overwhelming question," which is teatime.

And again the place is recalled. In the poem it becomes almost the haunting refrain that it is in the mind of the speaker.

Still finding comfort in time, the next section increases

the tension by raising the question of daring—only to particularize his fear. The tensional image of climbing stairs, with its implication of effort, only exposes his weakness in the self-conscious disabilities proper to un-romantic middle-age. Again there is the mock-heroic touch in his "collar mounting firmly," and the "assertion" of his simple pin. His fear has now mounted to the image of daring to "disturb the universe." And so he clings the more desperately to the comfort of time: in the possibilities of a "minute" he finds the courage to mention "decisions" where before he could only utter "indecisions."

In this projection of a psychological drama it will be noticed that Prufrock is coming ever nearer to "the room." Now he recalls the times that he has known, the trivial and timid measuring out of his "life with coffee spoons." At this point the imminence of his test is indicated by the emergence of the present tense: "I know the voices"; he is within sound, and presently within range of the other senses. He has known all this without doing what he now considers; so how should he presume to disturb the accepted order?

The images progress in intimacy as he approaches the climax: voices, eyes, arms. Now the eyes fix him, give him his place in the accepted order, with a formulated phrase. When he has been classified like an insect, how can he deny this classification and break with his past? How can he begin "to spit out all the butt-ends"—the violence of the metaphor has an appropriate indecorum for the social scene which intensifies the conflict within him.

As he itemizes the arms that he has known, he is distracted for a moment by an erotic symbol, the parenthetic observation "downed with light brown hair." He seeks the cause of this digression in "perfume from a dress"; but is it a digression? And if so, for the "you" or the "I"? Knowing these arms, he asks, "should I then presume?" The climax comes with a question which is also an answer: "And how should I begin?"

And begin he does, but he never finishes his proposal. After the preamble following "Shall I say," his psychological block sets in, and he concludes by observing the kind of creature he should have been—"a pair of ragged claws" in "silent seas," not Prufrock in a drawing room. It is noteworthy that his beginning about "lonely men" recalls the streets which he took on his way to the room. And the sea imagery should be kept in mind at the end of the poem. Eliot has indicated the crisis by typographical breaks in the text, but the transition is as simple as from "how begin" to "shall I say."

After this crisis the somnolent imagery is resumed and decreasing tension is at once marked. Of course the reversal is unfolded in terms of the tea party. Now the evening sleeps, or malingers, catlike, "here beside you and me"—both of whom, we must conclude, are Prufrock. For the lady is never "you" in the poem; she is "one." The rhyme of "ices" with "crisis" mocks their chime by their antithesis, and is characteristic of the way in which Eliot makes his rhyme functional. Now a series of heroic parallels, first suggested in Michelangelo, is begun in a self-justification which thereby becomes mock-heroic. Though he has prepared for his trial of strength, he is no prophet like John the Baptist; certainly not the hero of Wilde's *Salomé,* for he is "grown slightly bald." Though he has aspired to such a role, his self-consciousness makes him extremely sensitive to social discomfiture—reflected in the image of his head "brought in upon a platter," another likeness to John. And so his great moment has passed, and the "eternal Footman" of social fate—as inexorable as John's death—has snickered as he held his coat, dismissing him with the shame of inferiority added to defeat. Timidity has conquered his amorous self—the suppressed "you." In excusing himself he has seized on a parallel which both exposes and mocks his weakness.

Henceforth he looks back upon the event and rationalizes his failure: "would it have been worth it"? And always his fear of misunderstanding the lady and exposing himself to ridicule settles the question. To his frustrated self he explains that "among some talk of you and me" he might have revealed his buried life—here the Lazarus parallel expresses its momentous nature for him—only to expose himself to a rebuff. And the magic lantern image puts his great dread, public revelation of his sensitivity, into its most vivid form.

Then the poem turns again, this time to a note of decision, marking the resumption of his dominant role. He is not Prince Hamlet, though indecision might suggest it; rather the cautious attendant. Here even the sententious, choppy verse suggests the prudent character, as he takes refuge in self-mockery. The long, heavy sounds of weariness are heard in the line "I grow old . . . I grow old . . ." while he asserts the unromantic character to which he resigns himself, resolving, however, to be a little sportive in dress (by wearing his trousers cuffed). No more "overwhelming questions" for him; only whether to try to hide his baldness, or whether he dares to eat a peach. Perhaps all this will be his revolt against middle-aged decorum, but then the mermaids, like the lady, probably will not sing to him (as to Ulysses).

The imagery of the sea, begun with "oyster-shells," again emerges at this point; it is the imagery of his suppressed self. And the verse takes on a lyric or singing character where it has been talking verse before. The lyric note comes with the erotic imagery of the mermaids, and the hair of the waves recalls the down on the lady's arms. This watery, floating imagery involves the relaxation of all effort, offers a submerged fulfilment. It is ended when "human voices wake us, and we drown"— with the intrusion of reality, which drowns the inner life, the "us" in Prufrock. If this is a sublimation of the amorous Prufrock, it is a release of the timid Prufrock from the polite world which overcomes him. But reality returns, and the divided self is submerged again, not resolved.

Now we can see how Eliot has transposed his epigraph to a modern psychological context. Prufrock answers his suppressed self because "none ever did return alive from this depth"; hence he can answer without fear of being exposed. The reasons for this suppression, however, involve other fears. The "you" is the amorous self, the sex instinct, direct and forthright; but now suppressed by the timid self, finding at best evasive expression; always opposed by fear of the carnal, which motivates the defensive analogies. It is to this buried self that Prufrock addresses himself and excuses himself. His love song is the song of a being divided between passion and timidity; it is never sung in the real world. For this poem develops a theme of frustration, of emo‹ tional conflict, dramatized by the "you and I."

With respect to its poetic method, particularly its mode of connection, let us summarize a few of its characteristics. Evening likened to "a patient etherised upon a table" is not a logical inference, but an association or an intuition deriving from an emotional state; it tells us more about the perceiver than about the object of perception. The figure could be developed logically by observing the similar elements on each side, thus inferring the likeness from these signs. But the reference in Eliot's comparisons is less to the thing compared than to the mood, character, or situation with which it is associated.

On the other hand, "Let us go and make our visit" is followed by a logical inference—that of destination, for visits have destinations. But the inference is presented in the form of an image:

> In the room the women come and go
> Talking of Michelangelo.

And this image carries both the inference and a description—a description of place, by Eliot's favorite method of showing something happening there. But it also insinuates the mood of the speaker: at his destination they talk of Michelangelo; it is the first of his heroic juxtapositions.

Other things follow logically enough from this perceiver, his visit, and the room; but many connections in the poem are associative relations, not logical relations, and are established by the feeling, in which the association of images is an important factor. To put this method another way, it is psychological reference rather than grammatical. What is last in the mind (at least, previously) connects with what follows; in looking for the link we sometimes overlook the obvious. Violent breaks are violent only in the immediate context, not in the context of the poem, always the antecedent part. Incongruous elements are explained by the larger context of the poem. Never accept any explanation that conflicts with part of the context or with the whole poem. The explanation of violent or exaggerated phrasing must be sought in the character or feeling represented, not in the poet.

In general, metaphor and symbol replace direct statement in Eliot. In "Prufrock" we have what comes to be a familiar compound, observation, memory, and reflection, in which observation becomes symbol. The doctrine of the objective correlative means not only that the subjective is projected into the objective, or by means of it, but that it is expressed in other terms—metaphor; objects become symbols, and personal feeling is set apart from the poet. Connection through imagery is characteristic of Eliot, who is likely to exploit a kind of imagery, not to use it at random. A particular kind of imagery becomes the expression of a particular kind of feeling, not only in the same poem but in different poems. Recurrent imagery may not only reiterate a theme, but provide a base for variations, or development; its recurrence usually is accompanied by a deeper plumbing or a richer exploration of its significance. For some of these uses witness in "Prufrock" the sea imagery, hair imagery, sartorial imagery, that of polite versus crude society, that of bare sensitivity versus the protective shell, images of relaxation or concentration of effort or will, and finally the heroic parallels which both magnify and mock the overwhelming question.

Such a method of indirection is appropriate to a character who never really faces his inner conflict or his frustrated self, and hence is incapable of a direct expression of it, to say nothing of a solution. Here the most revealing lines in the poem are

> Is it perfume from a dress
> That makes me so digress?

But the observation "downed with light brown hair" is
no digression from the arms or from Prufrock's prob-
lem. This is why the epigraph, with its conditioned
response, provides an important clue to the intention
of the poem; and the title shifts its context significantly.
The title suggests the question for this song of indirec-
tion, made such by repression. The mock-heroic tone
is not merely in the author's treatment or in his charac-
ter's conception of the problem, but finally even in
Prufrock's evasion of himself.

Such a use of imagery is more than usually de-
pendent upon arrangement. But the order of parts will
reveal an implicit method in an Eliot poem that is
essential to its meaning. There is such a method in
"Prufrock"; it is begun by "Let us go" and ended with
"and we drown." The going is developed and drama-
tized even by verb tenses, the time element. The
"drown" submerges again what has emerged in the "go-
ing"—which is never directly said—and concludes the
imagery of his submerged life. To this arrangement the
author helps the reader in other ways. His punctuation,
for example, is functional, not conventional. What does
it tell you? Especially at critical points? Some of the
answers have already been suggested. Verse, too, is a
kind of punctuation, as Eliot has remarked, and he
comes to rely upon it more and more in this capacity.
Here the phrasal separation in the short lines may be
studied, and the effective chimes of the mock-heroic
rhyme.

All verse—even nonsense verse is not quite free—depends upon an order and organization capable of being followed and understood; requires an implicit, if not an explicit, logic—connections which can be discovered in the terms of the poem. If the words of a poem have syntax, they make sense, have a logic. Otherwise the poet has no control over his material except that exerted by metre. Only an ordered context can control the range of meaning set off by the single word; and relevance to this context must be the guide for any reader in determining the range of meaning or the logic involved. Empson's *Seven Types of Ambiguity* is a misleading book in that it explores possible meanings without proper regard to their limitation by the context. As George Herbert said, "the words apart are not Scripture, but a Dictionary"—for every context employs exclusion in order to turn the dictionary into scripture.

Portrait of a Lady

After "Prufrock" the "Portrait of a Lady" (1915) seems to be only another poem similar in form and theme. But it has a social malice which makes it more objective in attitude and more conversational in tone. Under a sophisticated surface Eliot develops a conflict of feelings which weaves its sensuous imagery into patterns of changing mood and significance. Yet it is not so much the portrait of a lady as the portrait of another uncertain Prufrock, adolescent rather than prematurely aged, suspended between feelings of attraction and repulsion. The epigraph from Marlowe's *Jew of Malta* (IV. i) suggests the situation, in which the dash after "committed" is important, for it indicates the moral uncertainty in the poem that parallels the uncertainty of accusation in the play. What this youth has committed is less certain than what Barabas committed.

This affair runs through a year, and the seasons are important to the development of its tone and theme. First of all the time measures the attraction, within which other feelings develop. The youth passes from a feeling of superiority to a feeling of uneasiness and uncertainty, which threatens altogether to displace the earlier feeling. In the first section, after the concert, the lady's approach and the youth's response are both developed in musical terms, which provide metaphors of malicious innuendo. These metaphors give polite expression to the lady and indicate the quality of reception in the youth. The implications of the lady's "music" set up a prelude in the youth's mind that is at least a definite false note, after which there is only one escape—the masculine escape to externals. The bathetic character of these externals of course mocks the confusion in his mind. It will be noticed how Eliot employs the dash to indicate a hiatus or sudden transition. So the section ends with the youth's attempt to escape the intimate atmosphere established by the lady, and the "tobacco trance" is his counter for the one she sought to induce. Of course the "atmosphere of Juliet's tomb"

becomes ironic in the love tryst prepared for this Romeo
by an older Juliet.

In the next section, now spring, the poet appropri-
ately adds flower imagery to the musical imagery in
developing the relationship which the lady calls "friend-
ship." This new imagery serves to intensify the feeling
of the lady and to make more intolerable the tension
of the youth. He still manages to smile and treat the
situation objectively, but it is proving more and more
disturbing. As he becomes increasingly preoccupied
with the problem

> The voice returns like the insistent out-of-tune
> Of a broken violin on an August afternoon.

As her "buried life" becomes more and more obtrusive
he becomes more and more uncomfortable, until flight
again is the only escape. But as the imagery of his
revulsion mounts so does her power to disturb him.
Thus he takes his hat rather than make "a cowardly
amends." But what does he mean? Does he mean, take
advantage of her? or has he done that already? Or does
he mean, to pretend what he does not feel? Either
means a cowardly escape from an awkward position;
and whatever his motive, his attention has given her
some claim. Certainly this section ends on the note of
moral perturbation. But the speaker has posed the prob-
lem of cowardly amends, and the poet does not change
the subject: what follows is a development of that
problem. If what the speaker reads in the paper char-
acterizes the young man who first sought to escape, it

also focuses his problem. The sensational items represent various kinds of desire and offense which do not disturb him. What does bother him returns in the musical and floral imagery which represents the lady and now combines in its qualities revulsion and attraction. Finally he poses the question whether his reactions to these things are right or wrong.

The third section answers the question by decision. His flight is no longer going to be temporary. But while his action is decisive enough, his reaction is shadowed with doubt. This time the imagery of his return involves mounting the stairs; and, as in "Prufrock," it is a tensional imagery of effort and awkwardness. Now his "self-possession gutters" in the candle imagery of the opening situation, and his smiles are really forced; he takes refuge in the objectively conventional, but his discomfiture is projected by his feeling of having to borrow the imitative actions of animals to find expression. And it all ends on the original theme of escape.

In imagined retrospect he contemplates her death after his going away—an event which would consummate the situation of the epigraph. But the issue is by no means certain, either in the rightness of his action or the quality of his feeling. The perplexity of his feelings is not resolved by this event, which seems to give her the emotional advantage and ironically to make her music successful. His final discomfiture is to become doubtful of "the right to smile."

What has he committed? Has he been tempted but

inhibited? Did he run away from a problem rather than solve it? Essentially the break between "committed" and "fornication" has developed into a theme of emotional frustration. He has been disturbed but baffled by the situation, and has been able to deal with it only by flight. Fornication is insufficient to characterize the action unless it includes the attraction and repulsion of sex complicated by moral feeling.

The form of this verse, Eliot tells us, was drawn from Laforgue and later Elizabethan drama, assimilating their conversational modes; its use of the half-line also reminds us of Spenser or Milton. It stretches, contracts, and distorts iambic pentameter and alexandrine verse; uses rhyme freely, functionally, not according to any set patterns. It develops verse as speech rather than verse as song, but the lyric note becomes insistent at times. It has the loose, repetitive, emergent syntax of speech, by which it becomes both reticent and insinuating. Note the syntax of the lady's speech when she is being most direct in her indirection, especially the anticipatory pronouns or loose reference which she clarifies as she seems to hesitate or feel her way along. These repetitive hesitations become part not only of the psychology but also of the speech as verse; they are imitations of speech that also function in the movement of the verse. And the verse usually quickens or beats more obviously when the youth is moved by the impulse to escape. The tonal quality of Eliot's verse is no less a part of the suppressed feeling of this poem, which is given a setting almost Whistleresque in its elegance of color. All of these elements contribute to the atmosphere or mood of the poem, which belongs to a world of revealing reticences.

For the experiments in imagery which we find in this first volume Eliot has a significant passage in his essay on Baudelaire. After remarking that in Baudelaire "the content of feeling is constantly bursting the receptacle," he observes: "His apparatus, by which I do not mean his command of words and rhythms, but his stock of imagery (and every poet's stock of imagery is circumscribed somewhere), is not wholly perdurable or adequate."[10] We are less concerned with imagery as "objective correlative" than with the particular stock that Eliot exploits in his early poems. After dismissing Baudelaire's more sensational imagery, he adds: "Furthermore, besides the stock of images which he used that seems already second-hand, he gave new possibilities to poetry in a new stock of imagery of contemporary life."[11] This was his real contribution, and it is highly significant to Eliot:

It is not merely in the use of imagery of common life, not merely in the use of imagery of the sordid life of a great metropolis, but in the elevation of such imagery to the *first intensity*—presenting it as it is, and yet making it represent something much more than itself—that Baudelaire has created a mode of release and expression for other men.

10. *Selected Essays,* p. 339.
11. *Ibid.,* p. 341.

We shall do well to reflect upon this passage if we are
to understand Eliot's own "apparatus" and his aspira-
tion in its use. This significance of Baudelaire for Eliot
is extended by one of his closing remarks:

> He has arrived at the perception that a woman must be to
> some extent a symbol; he did not arrive at the point of har-
> monizing his experience with his ideal needs. The comple-
> ment, and the correction to the *Journaux Intimes*, so far as
> they deal with the relations of man and woman, is the *Vita
> Nuova*, and the *Divine Comedy*. (*Ibid.*, p. 345.)

This is Eliot's own conviction, and we shall escape
error if we look for its consequences in his poetry, par-
ticularly when the women pass from image to symbol,
and especially when sex is involved.

In regarding imagery as the apparatus of expression
Eliot is thinking of it as the means by which feeling
is given form. To say that Baudelaire raised the sordid
imagery of the city to a new intensity is to say not
only that he made it convey something more than its
own sordidness, but that he explored it to new signifi-
cance, or found in it a release for the feelings which it
created. Thus he gave speech to other inhabitants of
the modern city, showed them the way to express the
new complex of feeling which their environment pro-
duced or the attenuation of their sensibilities in older
directions. And in teaching them how to formulate
their feeling he taught them how to exorcize it, how to
"cleanse the stuff'd bosom of that perilous stuff." But
this he did only for those to whom he gave a voice, not

an echo; for words must be made to express, not to
parrot, if they are to release. And Eliot also learned
to fuse the imagery of Baudelaire with that of Jacobean
drama, which had a similar capacity.

When he speaks of the elevation of common imagery
to the first intensity, he is not speaking as a neo-classi-
cist like Dr. Johnson, but of the perennial task of reno-
vating common speech for the expression of poetry, of
emotional accommodation between the ideal and the
real. As readers we shall profit if we notice not only the
stock of imagery with which he begins, but also any
alteration in that stock or his use of it. For when the
feeling, about death for example, alters, the imagery
alters. And we should notice not merely his selection
but his selection for intensification. Although this vol-
ume does not reveal the growth of larger poems from
smaller separate poems that subsequently become parts
of other poems, as later volumes do, it does show him
finding the means of expression for experience that is
subsequently realized in larger wholes or for parts of
experience that subsequently form new wholes. And the
clue to these genetic relationships, to his evolution of
feeling, is to be found in his imagery.

From this point of view his satiric observation of life,
which includes most of his early poetry, is less impor-
tant than the feelings which support it, or find expres-
sion in it. Here the shortcomings are less momentous
than the things they come short of. And we shall be
well advised to seek in this world of appearance the

hidden reality that matters. In general the objects of his satiric observation gall him at his most sensitive points; he does not write of things about which he does not care or has not cared. At first he would rather mock his own gods than have others mock them; later he is more prepared to suffer derision.

On the basis of imagery the poems of the first volume fall into two groups: that of commonplace imagery worked up to uncommon intensity, intensified by emotional selection; and that of esoteric imagery transforming common life, again under the compulsion of feeling. Or one might divide them into imagist poems, and poems of dramatic imagism, which develop complicated rather than simple feelings. Another way of putting it is to say that in one group we find static perception; no change of feeling in the perceiver, though his feeling may be emphasized by an opposite feeling; in the other we find dynamic perception: change of feeling or conflict of feeling in the perceiver. The latter type produces the more difficult poem. Though Eliot from the first draws upon musical analogy, it is erroneous to describe any of his poems as "the music of ideas." If ideas have music, they do not become poetry merely through the accidents of words. And to speak thus is only to evade the problem of order or form in a poem, unless you would make it tantamount to metrics. So the ordering of these images is no less important to their effect than their character, and the nature of that ordering differentiates the emotional patterns of the various poems. All of these experiments in imagery are really experiments in the objective correlative which Eliot defines in his essay on *Hamlet* and which is a natural consequence of his constant insistence in poetry on something perceived.

In "Preludes" (1915), which are preludes to various parts of the diurnal round, we should notice not only the emotional selection which heightens what is seen, but also how it is seen, for qualifying words intensify its significance. To the perceiver the objective becomes intensely subjective, an image reflecting a mind. "Morning at the Window" (1916) shows the two sorts of metaphor which Pound has distinguished merging into one another: "his wholly unrealizable, always apt, half ironic suggestion, and his precise realizable picture"; [12] or conceptual and perceptual metaphor. But the epithets qualify the perceiver's vision as well as their object.

Such poems of 1915 as "The Boston Evening Transcript," "Aunt Helen," and "Cousin Nancy" show how Boston affronted his sensibilities; they are caricatures of the genteel tradition. The stultifying world of "The Boston Evening Transcript," though it may sway in the winds of doctrine like its living opposite, is not so much ripe as dead. In "Aunt Helen" greater objectivity is achieved, for both the character of the aunt and the

12. See "Eliot" in *Instigations*.

attitude of the perceiver are reflected in the various effects of her death; the degrees of respect or disrespect are developed by antitheses. If the modernity of Cousin Nancy is not without its ludicrous touch, the tradition of the aunts is nothing if not "glazen," like the other "guardians of the faith." And it does not help their cause that the last line comes from Meredith's "Lucifer in Starlight."

Rhapsody on a Windy Night

More complicated feeling is expressed in another poem of 1915, which employs imagery of a more esoteric order. This is the "Rhapsody on a Windy Night," a title that in music suggests a composition of enthusiastic character but indefinite form. But if we take it as an effusion marked by extravagance of idea and expression, and without connected thought, we shall be coming short of the mark. This rhapsody has method enough; it concerns a windy night on a street "held in a lunar synthesis," and the speaker is returning to his lodgings. The lunar spell dissolves the usual order of the memory and provides a new principle of association; then time successively shakes the memory in an irrational but symbolic fashion, producing in each instance a synthesis which is both an emotion and a comment. The "lunar synthesis" gives a different ordering of things: the daily synthesis appears only at the end.

The street lamp measures the passage of time, is the director of the walk, becoming imperative, like duty, at the end. Each lamp spreads its ring and focuses the image; each time memories, freed from their ordinary relations, gather round that image and lend it a lunar significance. The woman and the moon are alike; and "the moon has lost her memory"—a fact which accounts for the dissolution of memory under her influence. Each time the image establishes the direction of the memory, gives the immediate principle of association. The last lamp brings memory back to the daily order, his lodging, responsibility, the usual routine—no less the "sordid images of which his soul was constituted"—and these are images that demand action, likewise automatic. His escape is cut off; it is the last painful twist of memory; this reorganization of the past has led fatalistically to the present. Where the comment has been implicit it now becomes explicit. The images have all been of twisted things that concentrate the horror of life. Release from ordered memory is not a release from horror, though "the moon holds no grudge."

This is a good poem to show how a principle of association, here introduced in the image focused by the street lamp, will give sense to what appears to be a series of discrete images. The principles by which Eliot's poems are ordered are always discoverable, if not explicitly announced, in his poems, and the mode of this poem is especially suggestive of his later developments. Its method of stating, developing, and resolving a theme describes a basic pattern in his formal experimentation. The reader will find the images of this poem, upon consideration, rich in interconnections. Space does not permit us to discuss the implications; if we can read the signs which mark the main route we shall at least know where we are going, if not all that we have seen. The criticism of Eliot often suffers from the fact that his critics are discussing only nominally the same poem; and if it is replied that this is as it should be, we can only object that such a loose agreement is not sufficient in other arguments.

Among the later poems of this volume "Conversation Galante" (1916) offers one of the simpler varieties of Laforgian dissonance. It is built on a sharp contrast of moods which mock one another. The eternal center of such conversations, insufficiently observed by the speaker, is indicated by the lady's remarks, which point his departures from the requirements. This poem suggests that Eliot responded to Laforgue's metaphysical bias before he learned to develop his own reactions to enemies of the Absolute.

Mr. Apollinax

The contrast in "Mr. Apollinax" (1916) is more wittily achieved, though it presents a different mixture of moods. The Greek epigraph, which is from Lucian's *Zeuxis and Antiochus,* merely points up an aspect of Mr. Apollinax that is apparent in the poem, though it is possible that the other aspect was also suggested by Lucian. Comments on a lecture supply the epigraph: "What novelty! By Hercules, what paradoxes! What an inventive man!" The essential paradox of Mr. Apollinax, the son of Apollo, is presented at once in what he suggests to the speaker, probably in allusion to Fragonard's "The Swing": the shy Fragilion and the gaping Priapus.

The various and contradictory impressions of his laughter are then developed in a series of images, which involve Proteus, the old man of the sea, who was prophetic and assumed various shapes. If the sea-imagery becomes a symbol of the release of the spirit, as in "Prufrock," it also merges into the imagery representing the rather unrestrained effect of Mr. Apollinax's laughter. The result is both to subvert and to release genteel decorum.

The cultural suggestions of the names in this poem are not to be missed, even if it is dangerous to define them. The addition of Cheetah to Channing is the broadest stroke. The general procedure of the poem is that each action of Apollinax is registered in a reaction in the speaker, always in an image; and these are finally set in contrast to the direct comments of the others, who are mystified by his paradoxes. But the speaker's impressions of his hosts are also given in images: he remembers them as just another tea. Thus Mr. Apollinax is presented as both shy and crude, intellectual and animal; and the combination baffles his host and hostess, to the amusement of the speaker, on this afternoon of a faun.

La Figlia Che Piange

The mixture of moods in "La Figlia Che Piange" (1916) is subtly and effectively integrated. In this vision of the weeping girl the cynical mood cannot expel the former emotion or dispel the aura of the experience. The Virgilian epigraph (*Aeneid* I, 327) recalls the encounter of Venus and Aeneas. Venus, disguised as a maiden asking "have you seen a sister of mine?" is addressed by Aeneas: "O maiden, how may I name thee?" This epitomizes the poem's problem of emotional recollection. In the first section we have the recreation of a vision involving beauty and pain, now beginning to be colored by cynicism—marked, for example, by "fugitive." His later, cynical, mood emerges clearly in the second section, as he defines the emotional values of the parting. As he remembers it now, it resembled the separation of body and soul in a figure which reserves grief for her and release for him, which translates pain into callousness. Then disillusion finds the "way incomparably light and deft," which unites them both in cynical understanding.

The last section records the bare reality in "she turned away," for she did not behave as first described, with romantic exaggeration. Yet he was, and still is, troubled. Though his later mood asserts itself in the reckoning of his loss, he is still troubled by the vision, its beauty and pain remain with him. Now he would mock or deny any emotional concern, but his efforts are vain. This vision of beauty involving pain that is subsequently qualified by disillusion reappears in the imagery which symbolizes mingled longing and frustration in his later poems. For the poet this becomes a central experience and symbol, like the symbolizing of woman which he finds in Dante and Baudelaire. It is imperative to mark the parallel. While it would be perilous to equate them, no clue to his symbols and their meaning is more important. "O maiden, how may I recall thee?" thus acquires an importance beyond this poem, posing a question of emotional harmony.

All of the more significant poems in this volume are Laforgian in their esoteric imagery, their mixture of mood and language, their ironic deployment. I have ignored the lines that are actually lifted from Laforgue, for that sort of borrowing has not the importance to understanding Eliot that is commonly given it. It becomes important, and Laforgian, only when it plays ironically over the surface of other poetry. Otherwise such borrowings can only be considered as integral parts of Eliot's poems, deriving their meaning from them. To interpret such borrowings by their original context is the surest way to discover that Eliot does not write pastiches. The influence of Laforgue, as Eliot remarks about influence in Pound, is apparent "more as an emotional attitude than in the technique of versification." At least this influence is not less positive in the ironic attitude which translates defections from the ideal into ironic sentiment than in the colloquial and symbolic technique of the verse.

Chapter *4*

ARA VOS PREC
OR POEMS 1920

The title of the English edition of this volume marks the first appearance of the Dante passage which has most compelled Eliot's imagination. He returns to it again and again. But Dante is both an early and a continuing influence; we may recall "Prufrock" or the dedication of the "Prufrock" volume. In that dedication the reticence of a foreign language concealed the seriousness of the author: "Now canst thou comprehend the measure of the love which warms me toward thee, when I forget our nothingness, and treat shades as a solid thing." [1] Without minimizing the earlier significance of Dante for Eliot, we can say that he has become a deeper influence as Eliot's own understanding has deepened—deeper and less obvious.

The title *Ara Vos Prec* no doubt strikes many readers as precious, but it is a sign of something more signifi-

1. *Purgatorio* 21:133-36.

cant. It carries us to the famous passage spoken by
Arnaut Daniel, master of the *trobar clus* or obscure
style of poetry. These are the first words of his petition,
"Now I pray you." [2] But it is not until much later that
Eliot's poetry dares to be, or succeeds in being, that
direct; hence their appearance here seems ironic, at
least a mocking ambiguity. If they now merely tantalize
the reader, or quietly flout him, they point a psycho-
logical direction which their borrower ultimately at-
tains, and the reader becomes "mindful in due time."
Now of course the poem to which such a petition is
most intimately related is "Gerontion," but it is not the
only cry for relief from pain. In general, however, this
cry finds even more indirect expression, and the mock-
ing surface continues to conceal the spiritual anguish
beneath; or perhaps it would be more accurate to say
that his feeling is complicated and uncertain, uncertain
of its final character and allegiance. The irony of Eliot
has more than one motive, and hence more than one
value, but it is never a superficial maneuver, designed
merely to disconcert the reader; it relates to a state
of feeling.

This volume continues the satiric vein; but it is con-
cerned not so much with social satire, or religious satire,
as with the plight of modern man; his institutions are
taken as signs, not causes, of his state of being. The
Sweeney myth is begun; Mr. Apollinax is now divided
into the shy intellectual and the bold vulgarian. Pru-

2. *Purgatorio* 26:145.

frock suppresses a similar duality, but the split now becomes explicit by dramatic separation into different characters. With this dual aspect of man Eliot is much concerned. Now he projects various human needs into the social scene with a sharp awareness of their past manifestations and a keen sensibility to their contemporary ironies.

The most significant formal development in this volume is the quatrain form, a singing rather than a conversational form of verse. Yet it becomes a temporary discipline rather than a lasting form. Much the same can be said for the French poems, which in general are rather more flippant. "Dans le Restaurant" is the important exception, for it is a new development of the "La Figlia" theme and a dramatic extension of the Prufrock mode. Both the French and the English poems probably owe something to the scoffing realism of Corbière. At least they seem to extend the irony of Laforgue into the sardonic humor of Corbière. But the chief new content for the Prufrock verse is found in that early masterpiece, "Gerontion."

The quatrain, of course, is a more compressed and disciplined form than he has thus far employed. Its limitations developed a more concentrated expression. The more concentrated it became, the more angular the speech; the gain in incisiveness was offset by a loss in musical utterance. If the close of "Sweeney Among the Nightingales" provides the exception, the rest of the poem proves the rule. The singing lyric has not proved to be Eliot's strength; the freer forms have given him more haunting expression. His use of contrast, which extends from the smallest to the largest element of poetry, now capitalizes on the symmetry—the stanzaic form—of verse, making it set off his antitheses. But he continues to use typographical indications of the inner form of his matter. In concentration of speech "Burbank" illustrates the extreme in his use of, even dependence upon, allusion.

1917 brought forth all the French poems—except "Dans le Restaurant"—as well as "The Hippopotamus," which owes some of its superficial aspects to Gautier. The other poems appeared in 1918 and 1919, "Gerontion" alone belonging to 1920. If the quatrains of "The Hippopotamus" owe any of their inflections to Gautier, it should be remembered that the octosyllabic quatrain is one of the triumphant forms of seventeenth century English verse. With ballad rhyme, this is the dominant form of this volume, which prepares the way for the medley of verse forms found in *The Waste Land*. And for that poem we shall reserve our discussion of "Dans le Restaurant" (1918), partly because of its sardonic *dédoublement*. The other poems we shall consider with varying degrees of attention, depending upon their significance.

The Hippopotamus

"The Hippopotamus" (1917) carries an epigraph from Colossians 4:16, relating to the "lukewarm" church, which is characterized in Revelation 3:14-18. The salient words in this character are, "I am rich . . . and have need of nothing." The hippopotamus, on the contrary, has need of so much; and the poem, which defines his relationship to the epigraph, becomes the epistle of the hippopotamus. Within the basic antithesis of the poem, that between the hippopotamus and the True Church, smaller antitheses are developed by the major opposites. For example, the hippopotamus seems firm but is frail, while the True Church presents no such opposition; yet this antithesis proves to be truer of the church. The wicked and derisive aptness with which each aspect of this antithesis is pursued need not detain us—and the rhymes and diminutives play their part—but the turn by which their major roles are reversed does require attention.

The hippopotamus's day inverts the usual order, but the church collapses it, and all because "God works in a mysterious way." As the "mysterious way" from Cowper's hymn describes the supernatural, its operation is inexplicable and unpredictable. And hence it gives us not only the satiric wonder of the sleeping church but also the sympathetic wonder of the limited hippopotamus taking wing. God's mysterious way provides the consummation of this poem, whereby the hippopotamus and the True Church exchange destinies and prove like their opposites where difference was expected. The hippopotamus seems to be solid matter and his ways materialistic, but not when compared to the True Church; the mysterious way which presumably explains the church can reverse their roles.

Among Eliot's works this poem is striking because it shows his first use of naïve imagery for ironic effect; he often draws upon the naïveté of the nursery tale to mark by contrast his disillusioned implication. Another part of the original epigraph for this poem, which is still retained in the American edition, derives from *St. Ignatius to the Trallians:*

> In like manner, let all reverence the Deacons as Jesus Christ, and the Bishop as the Father, and the Presbyters as the council of God, and the assembly of the Apostles. Without these there is no Church. Concerning all which I am persuaded that ye think after the same manner.

This emphasis on the institutional church is just as appropriate to the next poem to be considered.

Mr. Eliot's Sunday Morning Service

"Mr. Eliot's Sunday Morning Service" (1918) receives its orientation from an epigraph from *The Jew of Malta* (IV. i):

> Look, look, master, here comes two religious caterpillars.

The poem explores the possibilities of this statement relative to a Sunday morning service, particularly the union of religion and caterpillars. Left implicit is the injunction "Look, look, master," and you shall see. The first line, "Polyphiloprogenitive," is not merely a *tour de force*, but a learned word which derides the quality that unites the modern Church functionary with the caterpillar world. These very prolific, sapient, camp-following merchants of the Lord pass by the windows, preparatory to taking up the offering. The last line of the stanza brings the jarring contrast of now and then, quoting St. John 1:1, "In the beginning was the Word." The poem then explains how this came to pass.

"In the beginning was the Word, and the Word was with God, and the Word was God." Then a second or superinduced conception, a kind of over-fertilization, of the One (by Greek philosophy) produced Origen, and hence the Many with whom we began.[3] Origen as the causal link in this change of the one into the many, the Word into the sutlers, is characterized by "enervate," which telescopes his castration into weakness of doctrine.[4] This doctrinal weakness produced the commercialism in which "superfetation" goes on apace. But the original significance of the Word is still visible, within the Church, in the mural of the Baptized God; for the feet still shine in a disintegrating background.

---

3. Origen held that "in relation to God this Logos or Son was a copy of the original and as such inferior."
4. See Matthew 19:12 for the passage he misinterpreted.

With a reminder of the Paraclete, the Holy Spirit as intercessor, the descriptive characterization of the Church closes, and the action of the sutlers, of the service, is resumed. A break in the poem divides the Church and its service, emphasizes the present and the past.

Now the presbyters approach the aisle of penitence, and the young (for the sutlers are polyphiloprogenitive) are ready with their expiatory pennies, waiting "under the penitential gates." These, we are reminded, are "sustained by staring Seraphim"—as if we could forget the "red and pustular" young—but the souls, not the faces, of the devout "burn invisible and dim." The superfetation theme found in this part of the service now passes into the caterpillar world as the bee carries on the office of the presbyter, ironically replacing Christ as the epicene, and reflecting "enervate Origen." Pennies rather than pollen fertilize the relationship over which the presbyters officiate, but the likeness is there as well as the difference. If the Presbyter replaces the Paraclete as the go-between, Sweeney gets his baptism at home taking a bath, and suggesting in his actions the prime cause of this degradation of the Sunday morning service. For "the masters of the subtle schools," which began with Origen, "are controversial, polymath," more shifting than the water in his bath. The meaning of sapient in "sapient sutlers," first related to the Word, now comes full circle. Thus weakened theology has led to vulgar materialism, and the original significance of the Word, which is still visible in the mural, is translated into depraved counterparts of the mural.

No doubt the poet has presumed a little too much on erudition in the second stanza; but one is inclined to forgive him this malicious economy. It helps, no doubt, to know that Origen was ordained and deposed presbyter; that he adapted Greek philosophy, especially the Logos doctrine, to Christian thought, particularly to the Gospel of St. John; and thus subtilized, made controversial and polymath, the Christian religion. But without such knowledge it is possible, I think, to perceive that the epicene between God and man has been successively Christ, Origen, and Presbyters, not to mention the satiric metaphor. In the extremes of "enervate Origen" and vulgar materialism the satire presents another form of the Prufrock-Sweeney contrast. As satire it is directed against the same church as "The Hippopotamus," but its method is appropriately erudite rather than naïve, and it again strikes a revealing lyric note at the thought of "the unoffending feet."

Whispers of Immortality

"Whispers of Immortality" (1918) are not Wordsworth's "Intimations"; rather they are a little faint, perhaps clandestine, and their subject not wholly proper. By a sharp contrast, breaking the poem in two and deploying its elements, the attitude of Donne and Webster is set against that of the moderns. The pre sumption of the title is that we now have only "whispers of immortality," to which the poem ought to bear some relation. The initial statement that "Webster was much possessed by death" is followed by images which amplify the amorous aspect of possession. By experience he knew that thought embraces physical death while intensifying its lusts. Donne is another "who found no substitute for sense" in this apprehension. Knowing beyond experience, "he knew the anguish of the marrow," and that no fleshly contact could allay its fever; it burned for something beyond flesh.

In contrast we are much possessed by Grishkin, no "breastless creature," but giving "promise of pneumatic bliss," not ultimate bliss. Alien, overwhelming, animal, and rank, the flesh now dominates man. Even the "Abstract Entities," though abstracted from sense, are fascinated but fearful. But, says the climactic contrast,

> But our lot crawls between dry ribs
> To keep our metaphysics warm.

There is no marrow, no fever, in the bones; our fate is to fear any "contact possible to flesh"; hence an abstract conception of death must keep our metaphysics alive. Possessed by death, Webster and Donne saw beyond the flesh; possessed by flesh, we take refuge in abstractions to conceive any life beyond the physical. The challenge of Grishkin or the flesh to such ideas is the problem common to both parts, and the problem is not solved by the dry ribs of abstraction. Unlike Webster and Donne, we have to separate thought and sense;

otherwise living sense would conquer our feeble meta-physics. Our attitude gives us "whispers of immor-tality," for they are only the furtive rustling of dry bones.

Sweeney, whose myth this volume begins, has no such compunctions. The Sweeney myth deals on the vulgar level of boredom and horror with "birth and copulation and death," the most elemental facts. To Sweeney these facts have none of the subtlety which they have for Prufrock, but they are none the less dis-tracting or compelling; indeed, for him they are more relentless. Sweeney is the primitive in man, oblivious of and therefore unencumbered by culture.

Sweeney Among the Nightingales

In "Sweeney Among the Nightingales"—in which Eliot sought to create a sense of foreboding—Sweeney is threatened by death. From the beginning Sweeney is conceived as the ape man. Here as he laughs he pro-jects various suggestions of his animal relationship.

In this poem (1918) an attempt to seduce Sweeney in a café or public house is put into a framework that suggests the Agamemnon story, which provides the epigraph, his mortal cry, "Ay me! I am smitten with a mortal blow!" Sweeney, at first neither alert nor col-lected, rouses to danger and departs, but does not es-cape the net, for he leaves in the shadow of Agamemnon. Whether inebriated or merely sleepy, Sweeney's emergence from this yawning, dangerously relaxed state describes the turn in the poem which ironically culminates in disaster. This irony is marked by his passage from uncollected laughter to the collected grin, circumscribed by wistaria. Sweeney sprawls, gapes, is silent and heavy-eyed, until the bait of the fruit makes him "contract" and become alert. His refusal to take this sacrificial pawn reveals the change in his state of mind. The actions of the lady in the Spanish cape and the "murderous paws" of Rachel together spell out his danger. The agent of his fate is of course the "someone indistinct" with whom the host converses apart.

But the mounting tension of the poem is best observed in the symbolic imagery. After suggesting the animal character of Sweeney, the poem uses astronomical symbols to suggest the time, place, and portent of the situation. The constellations have ominous mythological associations, particularly of disaster at the hands of women. Sweeney keeps watch at the "hornèd gate" of death through lechery, the fate of the hunter Orion. Besides being associated with the Agamemnon story, the nightingale has its own bloody tale of betrayal, which Eliot uses elsewhere; and this reinforces the association with the Sacred Heart and the bloody wood. The blood imagery emerges with the fruit offering, for its color runs from the grapes through the wistaria and the Sacred Heart to the bloody wood, providing the inevitable dye for Sweeney. The "liquid siftings" of the nightingales—suggestive of the women—

provide a final, ironic but appropriate, stain for a tawdry tale.[5]

Most readers feel a lift in the poem when the night-ingales' singing is translated into the past "sang," for this shift brings the shuddering realization of Sweeney's connection with the ancient story. This juxtaposition also provides an implicit comment on both stories, marked by the ambiguous development of "liquid sift-ings," which pass from song to stain. Likewise the startling shift from the Sacred Heart to the bloody wood thrusts Sweeney's betrayal into an opposite moral context. The full import of Eliot's framework, by a char-acteristic device, now comes home, and it seems to be a little more than his avowed intention to create a sense of foreboding, a sense which he has given more abun-dantly to *Sweeney Agonistes*.

Sweeney Erect

"Sweeney Erect" (1919) is an ironic commentary on Emerson's definition of history, which supplies an im-portant parenthesis in the poem. Is the "lengthened shadow" that of man or anthropoid ape? Emerson's image of history is given a framework that makes the

---

5. *Plate:* Plata. *Raven:* constellation of Corvus. *Hornèd gate:* the gate of lechery or death (*Aeneid* VI). *Orion:* see constellation and myth; killed by Diana, sets in November; through Artemis (moon) connects with Agamemnon. *Gambit:* sacrifice pawn in chess. *Wistaria:* perhaps the purple web in both the nightingale and the Agamemnon story. Notice that the action of this poem sweeps forward in one long sentence.

shadow from past to present rather sardonic. There seems to be both contrast and parallel between Nausicaä and Polyphemus and the epileptic and Sweeney; the lengthened shadows of the former are not unequivocal, but they outline the poem.

The title already carries the simian suggestion for man, and perhaps a further suggestion. The epigraph from *The Maid's Tragedy* (II. ii) of Beaumont and Fletcher—originally spoken by the maid in a scene which suggests elements of this poem—here introduces another scene of "Sorrow's monument" for the wenches to see. Because there is more contrast between Nausicaä and the epileptic than between Polyphemus and Sweeney, the tragedy may still be presumed to center in the maid. Certainly the poem begins to paint a background similar to hers—translating desolation into epileptic seas—for the image which it substitutes for Emerson's. And in Ariadne it involves another maid's tragedy before including Nausicaä and Polyphemus as prototypes for the modern drama.

The latter characters are inserted parenthetically just as the poem begins to fill in the foreground, and thus make a transition to the modern scene. The stirring of feet and hands passes into the simian motions of the epileptic and Sweeney, who prolong and modify the "shadow of man." The victim of this history, the maid, has her behaviour variously interpreted. Sweeney calls it "female temperament"; the ladies of the corridor, feeling themselves involved, prudishly call it hysteria that might be misunderstood; Mrs. Turner is concerned for the reputation of her house; Doris, later an appropriate mate for Sweeney, treats it as a physical condition that will respond to stimulants. Sweeney's interpretation at least protects him against cutting himself with his razor. But his action and these interpretations are all part of what it means to see "Sweeney straddled in the sun" as a reflection of history. This image, by prolonging Polyphemus, transforms a maid's tragedy into an epileptic fit, and thereby provokes interpretations which leave her seizure as sordid as her foreground. It is a picture of horror, and this is the import of history when seen as "the silhouette of Sweeney."

Burbank with a Baedeker: Bleistein with a Cigar

While "Burbank with a Baedeker: Bleistein with a Cigar" (1919) suggests a cartoon, its epigraph is a complicated pastiche of more various tones than the poem itself. This epigraph is compounded out of these sources in succession: the snatch of song in Gautier's "Sur les Lagunes"—the motto on an emblematic candle in a St. Sebastian by Mantegna ("nothing is permanent unless divine; the rest is smoke")—*The Aspern Papers* by Henry James—Shakespeare's *Othello* (IV. ii) and Browning's "Toccata of Galuppi's"—the concluding directions of Marston's masque, "Entertainment of Alice, Dowager Countess of Derby." They summarize impressions of Venice which the poem attempts to project dramatically, by means of its two tourists. They indicate not only the kind of materials that came together to form this poem but also the disparate character of the impression, which adumbrates historical causes.

The poem itself contains other echoes, which pose a problem. We must distinguish between borrowing and allusion: the latter asks the reader to recall, since the reference is necesssary; the former does not. While borrowing may be reinforced by its reference, it may also be perverted. For example, nothing is gained by referring "defunctive music" back to Shakespeare's "Phoenix and the Turtle"; it merely functions in the necessary allusion to the passing of Antony's "genius" in Shakespeare's *Antony and Cleopatra* (IV. iii). This allusion puts Burbank's fall into the framework of that story with significant consequences. The location of Burbank's infatuation has already been established by the first two lines, which spell out Venice for most readers. And for Burbank, when dawn comes from the east, in appropriate mythology, the modern Cleopatra's barge continues to burn on the water.

Bleistein, who provides a contrasting point of view, is not romantic, but commercial; his type is not localized, "Chicago Semite Viennese," nor sensitive to local history. His eye has risen from the protozoic level to stare at a Canaletto, but it soon declines, like "the smoky candle end of time," for it has only commercial interests. "On the Rialto once" suggests Shakespeare's "Merchant" and other interests, but it has been undermined by commercialism. Money now opens all doors; melts the boatman and the Princess, who succumbs to a merchant prince, Sir Ferdinand—as the verse holds back his unromantic surname. He is, of course, the apotheosis of Bleistein.

On this decline of Venice—personified in the Princess of suggestive name—Burbank speculates, wondering who clipped its lions (St. Mark's), making them cleaner but less impressive. His meditation on "Time's ruins, and the seven laws" involves Ruskin's laws of growth and decay, which depend upon the morals of the age.[6] Thus an impression of Venice is conveyed through events; and we are obliged to conclude that if Bleistein is repulsive, Burbank is naïve, for Venice is more than either is prepared to see; "nothing is permanent unless divine."

A Cooking Egg

"A Cooking Egg" (1919) demands first of all that we recognize the meaning of its title; namely, the kind of egg used when the strictly fresh is not required. The epigraph is the opening lines of Villon's *Great Testament*, which date this testament, "In the thirtieth year of my age, When I have drunk all my shame." These lines also suggest the character of the testament; the

---

6. See *The Seven Lamps of Architecture* and *Stones of Venice*.

connection with a less than fresh egg is clear. It is beside the point that this was about the present author's age. Aside from the quatrains, this poem has an inner form that is externalized by typographical breaks. What is this form? It has three parts: the first presents a scene; the second looks to the future; the third looks to the past. But the second in looking to the future emphasizes what is lacking in the present scene; and the third in looking to the past emphasizes the hope that should now be realized, but is lacking in the first part and has been postponed in the second. In short, the first part presents his reality or immediate prospect; the second represents his unrealized hopes; and the third bewails their unfulfilment while he eats the shame of his reality.

Pipit has been regarded both as his old nurse and as a little girl, but the poem relates her to two capacities, bride and spiritual guide. Her name is that of a bird, named from its call note. She is old-fashioned, prim and proper; her sitting is archaic, "sate upright." Her knitting and her pictures sustain this character, which is emphasized by one touch of middle-class romance, "An *Invitation to the Dance,*" supported by daguerreotypes. The one object personal to the speaker in this room is *Views of the Oxford Colleges,* which evokes his past and the expectations that are developed in the second part.

When he reflects on what he shall not want in Heaven, we are reminded of the proper reference to earth and realize that he is speaking of his early hopes, now unrealized and deferred. Just as there is ambiguity in "want," meaning desire, lack, or need, so there is bitterness in the ironic exaggeration of his wants. When "I shall not want" reminds us of the twenty-third Psalm, this ironic exaggeration reminds us of "my cup runneth over." Of course the exaggeration also mocks the wants, even in the rhymes. Among these heroes Sir Alfred Mond and Madame Blavatsky belong to the contemporary world. It needs to be remembered that Madame Blavatsky was a Russian Theosophist and that Piccarda de Donati is a spiritual guide in Dante's *Paradiso* (III). Pipit seems to be his most realizable want, but she too will be useless in heaven, the scene of his unrealized hopes. Certainly she is prospective, if not actual, bride.

The third part brings us the lament for this state of things. The first melancholy question—itself a recollection—employs a device which Eliot has already used and is to use still more—a naïve image employed for its ironic disparity with the thing it represents. Here it is the "penny world" he bought so easily—the world of Honor, Capital, Society—to eat with Pipit in private. While "penny" may mock his naïve idea of achievement, it may also suggest the nature of the world he has indeed got. For the "red-eyed scavengers," collectors of the refuse of such hopes, are creeping to the city from their penny world. "Where are the eagles and the trumpets?" resumes and emphasizes prosodically the content of the first question, pointing the hope rather than the disillusion. And that hope is buried in an heroic image, suggesting both the height of the hope and the depth of the disappointment. The "red-eyed scavengers," whom he has joined, reach their destiny in the final lines, where they droop over crumpets, weeping for their lost trumpets, in a hundred tea-rooms of the Aerated Bread Company. This is the appropriate destiny of a cooking egg, where its products, alas, are not eaten behind a screen. Our hero has a penny world, but not the one he dreamed about in his naïve youth.

Allusions to Villon's *Great Testament* establish the character of the poem as well as the state of mind of the speaker. It is an ironical review of the past, and its mood is indicated by the epigraph. In Villon the lament begins with (st. 22) "I mourn the time of my youth," and then itemizes (st. 29), "Where are, etc. . . . ?" Eliot has used this scheme in his own way, and his use of contrast should prepare us to understand that way.

Gerontion

"Gerontion" (1920), meaning a little old man, is given an epigraph from Shakespeare's *Measure for Measure* (III. i). In the play the Duke as confessor tells the condemned man that life is not worth keeping; and (see epigraph) besides you never have it in reality, but pass it as in a dream. "What's yet in this That bears the name of life?" Whether Gerontion's life goes beyond the epigraph will appear in the poem. The opening lines place him in a comparable situation, and significantly a situation in which he is "waiting for rain." This phrase provides the theme to be developed. We shall see what it means, for it may turn out to be a symbol.

Let it suffice for the present that rain is life-renewing and is preceded by signs, for those who can read them. In the next lines response to the reading of the boy starts his thoughts, which are also relevant to his situation. He has known neither extreme of the book, neither the "hot gates" nor the "warm rain." If Thermopylae is involved in "hot gates," it merely extends the heroic suggestion. In his present abode the Jewish owner and his house coalesce; "the goat coughs at night" in a pasture described by the next line; "overhead" because the house is "under a windy knob" or hill. The "woman"— all the characters are generalized—performs the domestic duties, "poking the peevish" drain. When he summarizes his situation as "a dull head among windy spaces," we have yet to learn the meaning of his "dull head" and "windy spaces."

In this section, as in the sections to follow, some words need to be looked up, and others squeezed for their emotional qualifications. But here, as elsewhere in this book, the refinements of meaning must of necessity, and may properly, be left to the reader. It has been pointed out that the initial lines derive from A. C. Benson's *Edward FitzGerald,* but that makes little difference to the poem, which could not exist if it were no more than borrowings. Such borrowings will be pointed out only when they serve some purpose other than to account for the poem or its meaning.

The following section might qualify as a prime example of Eliot's alleged *non sequiturs,* but it is nothing of the sort. We may disregard the possibility that Polonius would agree that "a dull head among windy spaces" is very like a weather vane or might even be a sign. But undeniably rain does have signs, and the old man is waiting for rain. However, signs of weather are usually not taken for wonders; but in the context of the following quotation signs are so taken. This context is found in the Gospel of St. Matthew (12). But that source does not clarify this passage; hence we must turn to an intermediate source.

This source is a Nativity sermon by Lancelot Andrewes to which Eliot draws attention in his essay on Andrewes:

> Signs are taken for wonders. "Master, we would fain see a sign," that is a miracle. And in this sense it is a sign to wonder at. Indeed, every word here is a wonder. . . . *Verbum infans,* the Word without a word; the eternal Word not able to speak a word; a wonder sure. And . . . swaddled, a wonder too. He that takes the sea "and rolls it about with the swaddling bands of darkness";—He to come thus into clouts, Himself! [7]

Now, if we return to the poem, we can see that the passage in question has a sequence, which we might have trusted. For, following the request, the sign is given, of the infant Christ, the greatest of all signs of new life. But the sign is mute, not easily understood, "swaddled with darkness." Now the Andrewes passage is interest-

---

7. See *Seventeen Sermons on the Nativity* (London, n.d.), pp. 200-01.

ing chiefly for its illustration of Eliot's source of metaphor and of the way in which he can telescope his material. Once "sign" has translated its natural context into a spiritual context, it continues to function in the spiritual realm, without losing its natural reference.

In the "juvenescence" of the year the sign of new life manifested itself differently, "came Christ the tiger," an image of terror—or a springing form of terror and beauty, which anticipates the feeling of *The Waste Land*. Blake may be recalled, but this image derives from the unheroic speaker. "In depraved May"—depraved because of its more sensual beauty—came "dogwood and chestnut, flowering judas"; this sense of the corruption of spring or new life by ranker growth is supported by the passage in *The Education of Henry Adams* (Ch. 18). The sacrament of spring, both natural and spiritual, comes to be eaten, to be taken in communion "among whispers"—a phrase which introduces further depravation. It is perverted by Mr. Silvero, whose devotion turns from the Lord's supper to his porcelain at Limoges; by Hakagawa, who worships painting; by the Madame, who turns "medium"; and by the Fraülein, her client. The associative principle implicit in this passage is the perversion of devotion; and the action is universalized by a kind of exhaustive particularization, which includes the names of the characters. The break after "tiger," which is without a stop, marks the beginning of this depravation. Now Gerontion comments: "Vacant shuttles Weave the wind," not spiritual

reality. I have no haunting spirits, but I am a shuttle for
the wind, "An old man in a draughty house." The mean-
ing of "A dull head among windy spaces" is beginning
to unfold.

The next section, "After such knowledge," which re-
fers to the knowledge of the sign just given, poses the
problem of forgiveness. It is his apology to the Word,
but it generalizes his life into history. This is like a laby-
rinth or house full of false clues, where Ariadne's thread
is missed; the true are given either too soon or too late,
and are perverted either by courage or by fear. These
signs of remorse (tears) are forced "from the wrath-
bearing tree," his tree of knowledge, which now bears
the wrath of God. In this knowledge the particular tree
of the betrayer is the flowering judas. A peculiar, mount-
ing insistence in this passage derives from the isolation
of the imperatives to think at the end of lines, and a
similar haunting emphasis is given to other elements by
the same device. It calls to mind a comparable passage
in Donne's *Second Anniversary*.

Now when "the tiger springs in the new year, us he
devours." He comes to eat, not to be eaten. Having
made the great refusal, Gerontion must abide by the
natural order, in which time devours; only the super-
natural contravenes this order, and he is committed to
the order of death, not of life. Gerontion continues his
argument with the Word. "We have not reached conclu-
sion" about "what forgiveness?" when I die in a house
that is not my own—it has a Jewish owner. But he insists

that he has not made this show of himself purposelessly, nor yet from any excitement of fear. In this climactic section he may be reluctant to name the "you" to whom he explains or justifies himself, but his audience has not changed; it is still Christ, the sign of life. And he would be honest.

Here Eliot's borrowing from Middleton's *The Changeling* (V. iii) has sometimes perverted his meaning for readers. The next two lines state the whole spiritual change that has been developed in the poem:

I that was near your heart was removed therefrom
To lose beauty in terror, terror in inquisition.

These are the stages by which he was removed from the heart of Christ, for he has shown how he lost the beauty in terror, and the terror in inquisition. The questioning stage is developed in the history passage; the beauty and terror appear in the manifestation of the sign. In the inquisition stage he can only continue to question. He has lost the passion that brought him "near your heart"; but it would have been adulterated now anyhow. He has lost his five senses, but how would they bring him closer? We must remember that beauty was an aspect of his experience.

His senses resort to every device to "protract the profit of their chilled delirium"; thus they bring reconsidered sensuousness, like "reconsidered passion," but not closer contact. Now, instead of saying that the course of nature is not to be interrupted, he puts two

rhetorical questions which particularize the phenomena
he has just stated. Will the spider cease spinning out?
Will the weevil delay its destruction? Then this slow
diminution expands, with a kind of surging release, into
a violent image of destruction, carrying people—whose
various names internationalize or universalize them—
beyond the circuit of the Great Bear. "Shuddering"
marks the point of view of the observer, not of Callisto.
"In fractured atoms" makes this image an extension of
the destruction of the weevil. It may be recalled that in
Measure for Measure (III. i) the condemned man also
finds a powerful image of death: "And blown with rest-
less violence round about The pendant world." Thus
the "windy spaces" enlarge their significance.

We should remember that when the tiger "springs"
without his divine aspect, "us he devours." The gull,
also whirled in fractured atoms, is claimed by the Gulf,
as the old man wishes to be; yet he does not fancy him-
self as struggling against the wind, but "driven by the
Trades To a sleepy corner." The Trades, these winds
are his element as well as image of destruction, for he
has been a merchant seaman; but his way of destruction
is really that of the weevil. This conclusion may be re-
garded as an earlier variety of "Not with a bang but a
whimper," except that it is not bang versus whimper
but active struggle versus "an after dinner sleep"; it
recalls his initial lack of heroic experience. The final
separated lines again collapse man and house, and ex-
plicitly make the brain like the season, both in need of

rain. Thus "house" and "head" present the physical and mental aspects of one comprehensive symbol.

The unflinching honesty of this confession redeems it from utter hopelessness, for without such honesty no faith will be possible and there will be little hope in "waiting for rain." It should be observed that if this poem was suggested by the situation of FitzGerald, it is not exhausted by the predicament of his generation. In this poem Eliot opened a vein of feeling and imagery that he was not to exhaust for some time to come. Most of his poems before *Ash-Wednesday* continue to explore this vein. There was nothing adventitious about this, for he was plumbing ever more deeply his past experience.

Chapter 5

THE WASTE LAND AND
THE HOLLOW MEN

Some consideration of "Dans le Restaurant"
is relevant, if not imperative, to a discussion of *The
Waste Land,* not merely because its conclusion provides
the fourth part of the larger poem. Rather because, as I
venture to think, it is a conclusion in that poem also, the
dramatic conclusion to its negative movement. This con-
jecture and the fact that it was translated so as to form
a distinct part of the new poem suggest that there is a
similarity in the sequence of both poems. The nature of
this sequence first becomes clear in "Dans le Restau-
rant," but it is the negative development of the "La
Figlia" experience, which in that poem remains equivo-
cal.

A brief recapitulation of the development of "Dans le
Restaurant" must suffice. A dirty, debilitated, old waiter
becomes confidential with a diner, and tells the story of
his earliest sex experience. Incidentally, the reader will
do well to compare this poem with Eliot's explanation of
Dante's experience as reflected in his work. The *garçon*

begins by saying, "In my country it is the rainy season, with wind, fine sunshine, and rain; it is what we call the wash-day of the beggars." He describes the soaked and budding willows where one takes refuge in a shower. He was seven, and she younger. He tickled her to make her laugh; and he adds, "J'éprouvais un instant de puissance et de délire."

"But then, old lecher," interrupts the diner, "at that age!" The waiter continues that events are cruel. A big dog came to romp with them; he was frightened and had to stop midway. "It is a pity." "Mais alors," responds the diner, "you have your lust." Then the diner, who has shown disgust throughout, orders him to clean himself up, exclaiming, "By what right do you pay for experiences like mine?" He concludes by giving the waiter ten *sous* for the bathroom.

The last section of this poem, reproduced with slight changes as Part IV of *The Waste Land,* supplies the foreign old waiter with his ultimate cleansing. Phlebas, still the trading Phoenician, is drowned, deprived of his lust and greed. It was a painful fate, yet he "was once handsome and tall as you." But *The Waste Land* omits the cargo of tin, is not explicit about the painful fate, and less specific about passing the stages of his prior life. It adds details like "picked his bones in whispers"— a rather grim cleansing image—and specifies the audience as those "who turn the wheel and look to windward"—a homogeneous image of those who resemble Phlebas the sailor.

Now let us review the sequence of this experience in its elements. In the rainy season, when nature is renewed, Phlebas experienced the stirring of sex, and was giving it expression when he was frightened and frustrated. Later, in another country, he is debilitated, dirty, in need of "the wash-day of the beggars"; but he has this memory and his greed. Finally he is drowned, subjected to a painful cleansing, and we are reminded that he was once a fine figure of a man. This conclusion is reinforced by the action of his confidant, who gives him money for a bath because, despite his disgust, he has had similar experience. Hence we may infer that the experience is not regarded as unique, nor must its issue always be the same. Another issue is discussed in Eliot's essay on Dante.[1] And the ironic "*dédoublement* of the personality" reaches its most complex form in *The Waste Land,* but as defined in his essay on Blake (II).

The way of Phlebas and the way of Dante are the two opposite issues for the experience that first centers in "La Figlia Che Piange." We shall do well not to forget them when we are puzzled by the sex symbolism in Eliot.[2] Of course we cannot interpret *The Waste Land* by "Dans le Restaurant"; but neither can we ignore a poem which supplies a distinct part of another poem, including an important character, and otherwise resembles the later and more complicated poem. It may not be going too far to regard "Dans le Restaurant" (1918)

1. See *Selected Essays,* pp. 232-35.
2. See *Selected Essays,* pp. 117, 233-35, 343-44.

as an earlier exploration of the vein of thought and feeling that is plumbed in *The Waste Land.* The translation of part of it bears some testimony to its anticipation of the later verse, especially in its basic symbolism, to which "Gerontion" also contributed.

The Waste Land

In *The Waste Land* (1922) the experience of the old waiter becomes relevant to a whole land, at once the Fisher King myth and the modern reality. One may assume that the French poem was already behind the poet—four years separate their publication—when it suddenly fell into the larger scheme suggested by Jessie L. Weston's book on the Grail legend, *From Ritual to Romance.* The latent intention of *The Waste Land* might be called a reversal of Miss Weston's title—to translate romance back into its meaning as ritual. In her scheme the experience of sex, like that of Phlebas, assumes a universal or religious significance; it is connected with the state of the land. For the Vegetation myths erect the cycle of the seasons into a series of divinely ordered events; and this cycle of life is based on sex and personified in ritualistic figures. The fortune of the land depends upon the treatment of these figures, and thus upon religion.

To incorporate the individual into this scheme it is only necessary to parallel his experience with that of a figure in this ritual. The Fisher King in particular was both maimed sexually and restored magically. But one side of this experience can be paralleled in "Dans le Restaurant" and the other in the story beginning in Dante's *Vita Nuova.* Thus a twofold issue can be found in the experience of sex, providing a negative and a positive movement for *The Waste Land.* The most important idea for Eliot in Miss Weston's scheme was that the Grail story subsumes a number of myths; this provided him with both a central myth and a basic system of metaphor. Miss Weston argued that the meaning of the Grail legend centered in the Fisher King, and was explained by the Vegetation or Fertility rites. In this connection she called attention to the use of the Tarot pack, including the contrast between its present disrepute and its past authority. And she emphasized the importance of the Vegetation rites "as a factor in the evolution of religious consciousness" (p. 6). Of course this statement oversimplifies the elements which are compounded in this poem. Basically its myths have a common meaning, which permits their union; and this fact testifies to something permanent in human nature, which may be repeated in individual experience.

Before beginning our inspection of the poem, we must admit the fact that in its original form it was nearly twice as long. Ezra Pound reduced it to its present form, and Eliot has praised his performance.[3] This is the special point of the dedication, "For Ezra Pound *il miglior fabbro* (the better craftsman)"—Arnaut Dan-

---

3. See "Ezra Pound," *Poetry, A Magazine of Verse,* September, 1946.

iel again (*Purgatorio* 26:117). Obviously Eliot did not feel that violence had been done the essential form of the poem; certainly not that it was maimed. Hence this poem exists with the same sanction as his other poems; moreover, it does not pose a different order of problems. Only the publication of the original could dispute Eliot's judgment; meanwhile he rests on its present form. In one respect that form has changed slightly: the first paragraph of Part III was formerly two.[4]

This revision of the original may account for the notes attached to *The Waste Land,* or part of them. But what use is to be made of them? They identify sources upon which he has drawn, occasionally reproducing the pertinent passage; and they provide other information about the materials of the poem, sometimes including an opinion. So far as the recovery of this information is helpful to the reader, they may be used. But the effect of the poem cannot properly rely upon them, except as such effects are frustrated by lack of knowledge. Given the qualified reader, the poem must produce its effect without the notes. And qualification here does not mean recognition of every borrowing, but of borrowings which derive part of their effect from the shift in context.

The most important notes, however, are those which

---

4. In the notes two changes which were made after the 1925 collected *Poems* should be noticed: the note for line 312 has been moved from Part III to Part IV, and finally to lines 309-10, for they are "from St. Augustine's *Confessions*" (Bk. X). The final note now reads "our equivalent to this word" for "a feeble translation of the content of this. word." The removal of the implication cancels an earlier mood.

call attention to formal aspects of the poem, whether of character, theme, or plan. Of these none is more important, so far as poetic method is concerned, than those which relate lines to one another, or provide cross-references. These are not hints of the so-called musical organization of the poem; but, rather, significant relations or connections of experience. They indicate the operation of the subsumptive myth, its common themes or experiences and its interchangeable characters. Under this myth any parallel myth or any of its parts is a potential metaphor for other members of the same class; hence translations of one into another are both frequent and sudden, but neither wanton nor cynical. The effects of these translations, however, are complicated, often ironic, because of the differences between the contexts of the translated term. But these translations are possible only because of basic identities, which provide their real significance, though often by pointing up differences. They are not a series of paradoxes; they are not mere variations on a theme.

But let us consider what the prefatory note tells us. First, that three things were suggested by Miss Weston's book: the title, the plan, and much of the "incidental symbolism." Now the title draws its significance from the Fisher King story; therefore the plan of a poem with this title might be expected to relate to this story—the subsuming myth for Miss Weston's incorporation of Fertility ritual into the Grail legend. Likewise the "incidental symbolism" suggests the incorporated material.

which is supplemented from Frazer's *The Golden Bough.*
Finally, he speaks of the elucidation of the difficulties
of the poem, and for this purpose recommends Miss
Weston's book rather than his own notes. Many readers
have found neither very helpful. Let us remember first
that the sexual maiming and restoration of the Fisher
King is reflected in his land, and that when he is maimed
the land is waste; but most of all that it is a regeneration
story of a comprehensive kind.

The early note on the Tarot pack of cards shows how
comprehensive it became for Eliot; his manipulation of
the pack itself shows how he adapted it to that story
and incorporated other elements of his poem. This pack,
which Miss Weston had connected with the vegetation
or revival myth, is the chief key to his plan. It will be
noticed that death and revival are prominent in the
items mentioned in this note; and that his final arbitrary
association is "with the Fisher King himself," a turn of
phrase which suggests his central, if not archetypal,
character.

Now the Grail legend, as interpreted by Miss Weston,
connects the Lance and Grail, or sacred vessel of the
Last Supper, with the sex symbolism which is found in
the four suits of the Tarot pack. Thus the ceremonial
of the Grail, which has regeneration for its end, employs
means that are significant for both Christian and nature
rites. Its object, the Fisher King, is a symbol of repro-
ductive Nature, like the vegetation gods; having been
maimed like them, he has become the object of similar

rites; and it is to the volumes dealing with these gods that Eliot turns in *The Golden Bough*. But this king connects by his name with the Fish-Fisher symbols— an ancient Life symbolism, both pagan and Christian, which was based on the belief "that all life comes from the water." [5] And it is to get both the Hanged God and the Fisher King into the Tarot pack that Eliot modifies its associations, for it becomes the unifying device by which he tells the fortune of the modern world. Its original use, which appears degraded, "to predict the rise and fall of the waters which brought fertility to the land," is thus enlarged so as to include these associations, which are likewise centered in the idea of death and rebirth.

Miss Weston's treatment of the legend enables Eliot to see in the experience of sex the potentialities of the Fisher King and his Waste Land. In the poem the Fisher King is the prototype of the male characters who melt into one another, and his is the subsuming myth; hence the poem closes on him and his predicament, just as it develops after a comparable experience. He is the type who speaks throughout, even in the Tiresias interruption, which extends the speaker to include the other sex and to suggest the alternative consequences of blindness and vision. The same experience brought both to Tiresias. Some years later Eliot is explicit on the consummation of the lower love in the higher love, which alone can save sex from animalism; and distinguishes

5. See Weston, pp. 70, 126.

between Dante and Baudelaire on this basis. But at this time he had in Miss Weston the suggestion "that the Mystery ritual comprised a double initiation, the Lower, into the mysteries of generation, *i. e.*, of physical Life; the Higher, into the Spiritual Divine Life, where man is made one with God" (pp. 147, 172). This scheme could have provided him with a double level and a double issue for the experience of the poem.

Thus the poem becomes a kind of dramatic lyric, in which the lyric themes are projected by characters associated with the central experience, and the individual fortune becomes a general fortune. The basic experience is that of the Fisher King, which is made universal in Tiresias, and the central speaker comprehends not only the characters within the poem but the audience which he taunts. The speaker also is the "son of man," his inheritor; and this inheritance is the lot of the Fisher King, whose experience he repeats. This speaker, who is the subject of the fortune, is most constantly related to Ferdinand, Prince of Naples. But, needless to say, Ferdinand as potential Fisher King is not Shakespeare's character, for he hears a very different music and it brings him to a very different vision. Yet the contrast is not without its advantage, for Eliot uses him as a link between magical and modern experience, recalling the Miranda vision. Ferdinand combines the roles of the Sailor and the Fisher King, or mediates between them. While both represent the same disablement by sex, they also suggest different issues of this experience. For this

division Eliot may have found support in the double
initiation of the Mystery ritual, with the first of which
Miss Weston associated "the horrors of physical death."
But Eliot makes death a consequence, not a test, for the
first—unless it is completed by the second. As a modern
knight of this legend, Ferdinand is a victim rather than
a restorer, and this role is foreshadowed by another
change.

At the beginning of *The Waste Land* we notice a fun-
damental, indeed instrumental, difference in Eliot's use
of the vegetation myths. In these myths the appropriate
attitude towards the renewal of life, or spring, is one of
rejoicing; here it is the reverse. Aside from these myths,
this attitude strikes the reader as a paradox in English
poetry; in relation to these myths, it is fundamental to
the meaning of the poem. The people of the Waste
Land are not made happy by the return of spring, of
fruitfulness to the soil; they prefer the barrenness of
winter or the dead season. On the psychological level,
the sex level of the myths, the same attitudes are evi-
dent. This reorientation should never be forgotten in
the poem; it is indispensable not only to the meaning
of the whole but also to the reference of particular
parts. For example, it is evident in the general attitude
toward water, the life-giving element of the myth; and
of course explains the use of water. Where water ap-
pears as desirable, it is only in recognition of a terrible
need. One is more likely to drown in it as the vital prin-
ciple than to slake his thirst by its symbolic meaning;

hence its connection with both sex and religion. Miss Weston provided a hint for developing the different aspects of water when she opposed the belief "that all life comes from the water" to "a more sensual and less abstract idea" that connected "the Fish with the goddess Astarte or Atargatis" (p. 126). When the lack of water is felt, it assumes a positive character; but for the most part it is negative or something to be feared. This is a logical consequence of Eliot's inversion of the vegetation myth, which makes the inhabitants of the Waste Land fear the return of life. And this reversal enables him to express the theme of religious frustration in terms of the myth which subsumes so many myths, for sex can be seen as both the origin and frustration of life.

It is a mistake to say that the poem "exhibits no progression" and ends where it began. The fear which the speaker promised to show is exhibited in its full course and ultimate potentiality. From one point of view it is a tremendous compression of human history; from another it is an equally startling expansion of "Dans le Restaurant." In a poem so compactly organized, it is necessary to form some idea of its basic scheme; in a poem so full of symbolic translation, it is imperative to keep our eye on the term that is translated. Hence we shall give our attention first to the relation of the parts to a basic scheme, and then to the connection of themes within and between the parts. Our purpose, as before, will be to see what the poem is about in its simple and immediate sense.

As the title indicates the myth of the Waste Land, so that myth gives meaning to the protagonist. We have already noticed how Eliot accommodated the Tarot pack to this myth, since the Tarot is his chief means of exploiting it. Hence this myth, as implemented by the cards which appear in the fortune, should provide the basic reference for the parts of the poem. In this myth we have noticed that the Waste Land owes its condition to the disability of the Fisher King, who thus resembles the vegetation god. But Eliot has introduced both the Fisher King and the Hanged God into the Tarot pack, and hence wishes to keep their roles separate.

In fact, though both were victims, the Hanged God, whom the Madame does not find, represents in the poem the final cause of the Waste Land and its possible restoration. In legend he was sacrificed in order that nature might be renewed. Now "The Burial of the Dead" relates primarily to him, and the state of the land is an effect of his death. Any change in that state is contingent upon his revival, but also upon the attitude of the people. The Fisher King's role is to represent man's fate as it originates in sex but cannot transcend it; without this transcendence, which is figured in the Hanged God, he is doomed to death. The Fisher King is differentiated from the Phoenician Sailor by his awareness of the means of transcendence. Hence the first part of the poem develops the death theme, for god and man, and relates the fear of it to sex, as in the myth.

In the second part the protagonist, whose association with the Phoenician Sailor is made to suggest Ferdinand, encounters "Belladonna, the Lady of the Rocks." Her attraction for him and her danger to a sailor are both suggested by her names. Now life as the sex game is sterile, like the land. In "A Game of Chess" sex as the death principle is exposed on two levels of society. Here, both by text and by note, the reader is forcibly reminded of the garden experience and the fortune of Part I, the effects of which appear in the protagonist.

"The Fire Sermon" brings the Merchant of the fortune, with suggestions of his mergence with the Sailor. The music which creeps by Ferdinand upon the waters of Leman develops the lust or death theme, reveals its moral significance, and suggests its moral need. Since his fate has been connected with water, water has assumed a fateful attraction for the protagonist, who both fears and craves it. In terms of the fortune the course of these waters is highly significant.

"Death by Water" brings the Phoenician Sailor and the ultimate consequence of the lust theme, of the fire. Now the protagonist's anticipated fate has been executed. But some elements of his fortune have not yet appeared, and hence some of its meaning remains to be unfolded.

In "What the Thunder Said" these elements appear, in a continuation of the scene which originally evoked the Waste Land and in an intensification of its terrible need. The Hanged Man becomes more explicit, and is associated with the "hooded figure" in the passage to Emmaus. Now the "crowds of people" take on substance, and the Fisher King, like the Hanged Man, becomes more distinct in the Man with Three Staves. To these, as to the dead Sailor, the opening theme is relevant; for the Thunder, as herald of spring, speaks of revival. Death has become an agony; and, after his journey through the Waste Land, the protagonist is given by the Thunder three staves which could make revival possible. But, once more fishing, he prepares for death, his fate; and describes his situation by means of the fragments, the "broken images" of Part I, which he has shored against his ruins. And death is the ultimate meaning of the Waste Land for a people to whom its explanation is only a myth, for whom sex is destructive rather than creative, and in whom the will to believe is frustrated by the fear of life.

At this point it will perhaps be sufficient merely to cite an omission till now, the epigraph of the poem. Its source is the *Satyricon* (Ch. 48) of Petronius, and its speaker is Trimalchio, a wealthy and vulgar freedman: "With my own eyes I saw the Sibyl suspended in a glass bottle at Cumae, and when the boys said to her: 'Sibyl, what is the matter?' she would always respond: 'I yearn to die.'" This ironic situation is matched in that of Madame Sosostris; both conceal a deeper meaning, and both seem to mock it. Perhaps we can point to the center of this effect in Eliot's poem. Reduced to its simplest terms, *The Waste Land* is a statement of the experience that drives a character to the fortune-teller, the fortune that is told, and the unfolding of that fortune. But this latent narrative is both universalized and greatly complicated by being set in a framework of the legend in which Miss Weston had seen so many myths. And the poem follows the cycle of its torment, from spring to spring, the time of Easter—a religious festival of great antiquity. The realism of the poem brings it into Baudelaire's symbolic "mode of release and expression" as defined by Eliot: "not merely in the use of imagery of the sordid life of a great metropolis, but in the elevation of such imagery to the *first intensity*—presenting it as it is, and yet making it represent something much more than itself."

1

The paradox of the seasons, with which the poem begins, inverts the normal attitude towards the life-cycle, thus reversing the significance of the vegetation myth and giving an ironic turn to the office of "The Burial of the Dead." Spring disturbs the dead land, stirring memory and desire; winter lets it forget. Then the verse modulates into narrative, the stirred memory that illustrates and supports this attitude. Summer caught them unaware (surprised them), coming with rain. If it were not for the opening lines, this would seem little more than an international episode—a memory of another spring. In this garden scene Marie is introduced by the

German, "I am not Russian, I come from Lithuania,
pure German." Her desire for the mountains is mixed
with a memory of fear, and her life is a retreat.

But what are the dull roots to be stirred by rain? The
son of man cannot answer because he knows only the
Waste Land, which here suggests both the death im-
agery from Ecclesiastes and the fear "of that which is
high" illustrated in Marie. Here Ecclesiastes 12 blends
images from Isaiah 32 and Luke 23: latent in the "dead
tree" and the "red rock"—the color of "The Fire Ser-
mon"—is the burial of Christ, which involves the pre-
server of the Grail (Joseph of Arimathæa) and brings
the journey to Emmaus in Part V. The speaker, who
often echoes the prophetic note, will show man some-
thing different from the shadow of time in this land; he
will show him "fear in a handful of dust." If this image
begins with the Biblical association, it ends in the vege-
tation myths. And again we get a garden scene, framed
by the sailor's melancholy song in *Tristan*,[6] a story of
tragic passion. The question "where lingerest thou?" is
finally answered by "desolate and empty the sea." But
the garden scene accounts for the answer. The capital-
ized Hyacinth suggests the vegetation god and a victim
of love. The protagonist's response is striking: a failure
of speech and sight, a state neither living nor dead, de-
scribing the effect of the vision of the Grail upon the

6. The opening German has been translated thus:
"Fresh blows the wind from off the bow,
My Irish maid, where lingerest thou?"

impure. A love-death would be appropriately framed by snatches of song from Wagner's *Tristan und Isolde*, but the sea in itself expresses a sufficient change. The German carries us back to the scene with Marie and amplifies its associations.

Eliot's references to the present scene in Part II make it very important. Its final meaning, what is to be discovered in "the heart of light, the silence," remains to be seen. Let us remember that we were to be shown fear; the associations of this experience acquire a new setting in the fortune. For the moment we may venture this statement: the initial state of mind is defined by the experience of spring followed by the experience of the Waste Land; "the roots that clutch" in both are those of fear, and their origin is found in the "Hyacinth garden."

The speaker's need of clairvoyance introduces Madame Sosostris; perhaps she can look into the silence and interpret. She is a psychic fortune-teller, but she has a bad cold, which may hamper her powers; nevertheless, her wisdom is the best there is, involving a malicious pack of cards. The fortune itself has already entered our discussion, and accounts for the rest of the poem; but some details may be observed. In general her limitations, and the irony of the poem, appear in what she does not see. Her clairvoyance does not extend to an identification of the protagonist with Ferdinand, but only with the drowned Phoenician Sailor; yet the line from *The Tempest* which suggests this identification also connects the "pearls that were his eyes" with the preceding experience, "my eyes failed." Of course this is a transformation image, which in the present context is committed to death. The irony of her shortcomings is more apparent in the failures to see which she mentions. In fact, the voice of irony begins to be heard in this section. In terms of these cards (but not of the initial attitude) there is none greater than to "fear death by water." If "dear Mrs. Equitone" is the lady of nerves in Part II, we may add to the irony. Certainly we must not forget it in the line, "One must be so careful these days" —lest this wisdom fall into the wrong hands. But the fundamental irony is the restoration of a greater meaning to life by means of this "wicked pack of cards."

Henceforth this fortune and the experience which it interprets color the vision of the protagonist. Although he has become one of the dead—"I had not thought death had undone so many"—the city appears "unreal" to him as it does not to them. They do not share his misgivings about the Waste Land; they are not conscious of the cruelty of April or of "a dead sound on the final stroke of nine" (Luke 23:44). He not only confuses but mingles his fortune with their reality. This explains the illusionary aspect of the poem, which assumes the Hamlet mask of irony or madness when the apparent contrast seems too great. Death echoes through this section until it culminates in "That corpse you planted last year in your garden." You do not plant corpses, except in vegetation ceremonies; and we are reminded of the "Hyacinth garden," of the slain Hyacinth and the garden experience. The taunting questions about the expectation of growth intimate that this was not so much a planting as "the burial of the dead." And the "hypocritical reader," as well as Stetson and the speaker, engaged in this planting of the corpse which evokes the corn-god Osiris, the scattered god of resurrection, and suggests the Hanged Man, whom the Madame did not find. The sardonic tone of the speaker has behind it not only this awareness but the weight of his own experience in the garden, of his attitude towards the seasons, and of his fortune. The corpse of the garden appears again in Part V, where this theme is openly resumed.

But one or two details in this section cannot be ignored. When the protagonist mentions "the ships at Mylae," he is associating himself, appropriately enough, with the Phoenician Sailor in a famous engagement of the Punic Wars. We should note the associations with the sea and things Phoenician in the poem; they are part of the protagonist's inheritance. The "Dog" is more important than Eliot's transformation of Webster; rather, it is the transformation, for it develops the ambiguity of the planted corpse. If Dog involves Sirius—as in "Sweeney Among the Nightingales"—he becomes a sign of the rising of the waters and is friendly to growth. But Dog may also involve Anubis, guardian of the dead, who helped to embalm the broken Osiris. By his ambiguity the Dog presents an ironical aspect, and this irony centers in the intent of the planting, which explains the "hypocrite lecteur" and his ambiguity as both subject and object. We must not ignore Eliot's use of capitals. As a source the dirge in *The White Devil* (V. iv) is significant because it provides a suggestive parallel and contrast with the dirge from *The Tempest,* which describes the drowned Phoenician Sailor; and because it belongs to a scene which recalls the mad Ophelia and includes a ghost with a flower-pot containing "A dead man's skull beneath the roots of flowers." This is Eliot's most Websterian poem, not least in the imagery. And let us observe that the ironic close which is found in Part I is repeated in other parts. If the Dog and the Hyacinth garden generalize the memory of "Dans le Restaurant," they illustrate the extension of that poem.

II

Of the rich allusiveness of the opening section of Part II, much is indicated in the notes, and much has been said. In its opulent detail "the lady of situations" issues from a long past into a luxurious present. Egyptian Cleopatra and Phoenician Dido suggest her varied fortunes, and their splendor surrounds her, touched now and then by a sly detail like the parenthesis. Most insinuating, however, are "her strange synthetic perfumes," which "troubled, confused And drowned the sense"; for here we are in the presence of Belladonna, no less narcotic than cosmetic, herself presently in need of an ano-

dyne. But as a Siren she is more than a parody of Pater's
Mona Lisa. The pictured "change of Philomel," whose
place in Part III is indicated by a note, introduces an-
other significance in the suggestion of violation sur-
vived by the "inviolable voice."

> And still she cried, and still the world pursues,
> "Jug Jug" to dirty ears.

The chase has not ceased, and the nightingale's sounds
are both representative Elizabethan and associative
modern. If the other pictures are "withered stumps,"
like Philomel's tongue, they come into the class of
"broken images"; but at least provide an inclination,
"leaning, hushing the room enclosed." As someone ap-
proaches, the lady's hair becomes a sensuous and irri-
table image of her mood.

Then as she speaks we are reminded of the garden
experience, for her questions counterpoint "I could not
speak." The protagonist is thinking about "rats' alley,"
the waste alley of death; and a note connects it with
Part III. If the borrowing from Webster's *Devil's Law-
Case* (III. ii) is looked up, it will only reinforce the
Websterian character of this scene. But the wind's part
in this poem bears inspection. The questions about
knowing, seeing, and remembering nothing play over
past details as the memory comes. We remember "my
eyes failed . . . and I knew nothing" as he recalls his
"death"; and a note connects it with the garden and
fortune. Of course his replies puzzle the lady until she
asks if there is nothing in his head. And he answers,

nothing "But O O O O that Shakespeherian Rag"—only the tune of Ariel's dirge. While he mocks, she becomes the image of distraction; and her ultimate question is answered by his derisive but grim summary of the daily boredom waiting for the final knock. Eliot's reference to Middleton's play merely emphasizes the game of chess as a cover for seduction, especially for "the lady of situations" in the upper class.

The change of speech in the next section immediately places the scene on a lower level of society. But to place it in a "pub" or tavern, we need to recognize "Hurry up please its time" as the words which announce its closing time. This scene makes explicit, without the reticence of the other's game, what is meant by "a good time." And it does this in verse that not only catches the inflections of the lower class, but shows time hurrying it along instead of hanging upon its hands. The problem which appears in Lou's or May's gossip comes to a climax in the question, "What you get married for if you don't want children?" It puts "a good time" against a background of the frustration of life, and modulates the death theme to this level. The final "good night"—ironic in its elegant, ceremonious contrast—is in the language of the first scene, and derives from Ophelia's mad farewell (*Hamlet,* IV. v.); hence the protagonist did not stay with the lady of nerves, but is still mocking the lady of situations with bits of "Shakespeherian Rag," as he recalls another death by water. If this is a very economical rounding-off of both scenes,

it is not a departure from Eliot's manner of making
his speaker identify himself, and certainly not from the
particular means of discrimination employed in this
part.

III

"The Fire Sermon" not only extends "A Game of
Chess" but exposes its moral significance. It is devel-
oped likewise in terms of the obsessions which derive
from the protagonist's fortune. What haunted his mind
in the previous part now centers his vision, "death by
water," which is associated with the characters that
develop its ominous implications. Here we find the
Merchant who melts into the Sailor and "the Lady of
the Rocks," but in the midst of all the river. The dead
season has come to the river; its canopy of leaves is
broken:

> the last fingers of leaf
> Clutch and sink into the wet bank.

And so do all who live by this river, which ultimately
flows into the sea that drowns the Phoenician Sailor.
The "Sweet Thames" refrain, which derives from Spen-
ser's *Prothalamium,* reminds us of "A Spousall Verse"
and announces another song. The title has warned us
that there is a sermon in the song, and both indicate
that this part will be more evocative than dramatic.
After the reminder of Spenser, the description of
the river suggests that his song is being rewritten in

a modern key; and this suggestion is reinforced by
the transition from the "nymphs" to their "friends,"
who have been casual indeed, "left no addresses."
Then comes the sudden revelation, both of the waters
and the mood:

> By the waters of Leman I sat down and wept . . .

This line is reinforced by remembering Psalm 137:
"By the rivers of Babylon, there we sat down, yea,
we wept, when we remembered Zion." But why the
change to "Leman"? Not because it is the old name
for Lake Geneva, but because it is an old name for
"lover." Water in the modern Waste Land is a nega-
tive element, a river of lust. After this apparent but
not real *non sequitur,* he reinvokes the Thames. The
request to "run softly till I end my song" may acquire
further meaning.

The next lines, after the method of this poem, iden-
tify the speaker by his thought. The sounds of death
haunt the protagonist with whom we have been con-
cerned. He is not the poet, unless we choose to ignore
all of his efforts to project a character by means of a
series of illusory characters. Now he hears Marvell's
figure of time as a figure of death, and is once more
in "rats' alley" as the one who wept at Ariel's dirge.
But Ferdinand is modernized; he is not merely

> Sitting on a bank
> Weeping again the King my father's wrack.

And he is also more ancient than Ferdinand; he belongs to the line of Fisher Kings. It was while sitting on this bank that Ferdinand heard Ariel's dirge—now fixed in the protagonist's mind by its association with the Phoenician Sailor. Before long he echoes the line which completes this quotation, but meanwhile much has intervened to reinterpret "this music."

But at his back he hears other sounds—or are they different? They are the sounds of the city, but in a familiar pursuit. They are the modern sounds of hunting, of lust; whether it is "Actaeon to Diana," or "Sweeney to Mrs. Porter," it is the old game of Tereus and Philomel. To the protagonist, whether he would be a Parsifal or is to be a Fisher King, washing the feet is a spring rite in another sense, for it preceded the restoration of the Fisher King and was accompanied by the singing of children in the choir loft ("And O! those voices of children, singing in the cupola!"). The irony belongs to his vision: water has lost its proper efficacy, has become malignant. But the choir melts into other sounds that carry a theme—the song of rape belonging to the nightingale, already introduced.[7]

"Unreal City" indeed to such a vision, to a mind concerned with the Fisher King! Of course the implication is that it lacks true reality. On the realistic side, how-

---

7. See Trico's Song in Lyly's *Campaspe:*
What bird so sings, yet so does wail?
O! 'tis the ravished nightingale.
Jug, Jug, Jug, Jug, Tereu, she cries,
And still her woes at midnight rise.

ever, it appears unreal "Under the brown fog of a winter noon."

Whether the name of the Merchant plays on the meaning of "well-born" or not, he is now unkempt; and reminds us, particularly by his vulgar French, of the old waiter in "Dans le Restaurant." Perhaps that poem has given us both the Merchant and the Sailor, who coalesce. If he has made improper advances to the protagonist, which would support the general lust theme, he is still the trader; and business is probably the rival mystery which the Madame is forbidden to see, despite her discreet "Thank you." This would explain the use of cryptic business terms. Of course they may be subordinate to the "currants" as dried vestiges of the Bacchic cults, and thus part of an initiation into similar orgies, or merely of an initiation into the modern ritual, involving a sight draft. Miss Weston (p. 160) stresses the importance of such traders in spreading the Attis cults. But "profit and loss" is an important sign in the mergence of Merchant and Sailor, and must not be discounted, even as a Phoenician lust. Thus the loss of vision passes from the garden to the fortune to this embodiment.

If the sequence carries us from the "one-eyed" to the blind, it does not leave the hunt of lust in the city; and if the protagonist has now been qualified in the knowledge of both sexes, he is ready to assume the role of Tiresias. He has already sounded the prophetic note "by the waters of Leman," and the "motors" now pass into the "human engine," which expresses itself mechanically. "I Tiresias" is the only explicit identification of the speaker in the poem, and there is a reason for it. He is not a character in the fortune; but he is the supreme metamorphosis that brings together all the metaphoric transformations and thus is qualified to summarize their experience. "What Tiresias *sees,* in fact, is the substance of the poem," but not the whole poem.[8] This departure from the fortune is therefore identified. And for the protagonist the sexual qualifications of Tiresias have a deeper meaning than prophetic power: he, "though blind," is "throbbing between two lives," one dead, the other powerless to be born. But, like Tiresias, he can see the nature of the "dead"; his vision springs from similar experience.

The introduction of "the typist" illustrates Eliot's device of syntactic condensation; functioning as both object and subject, she exemplifies the metamorphic flow of things in this poem. The typist scene repeats on still another level, and still more openly, the "game of chess" episode; but, more significantly, it interprets bluntly this experience for the participants. They are apathetic, both morally and emotionally—human machines. The role of Tiresias is also appropriate to the protagonist because he is now walking "among the lowest of the dead." Finally the modern significance of this act is registered in the reaction of the typist; the

8. A later statement of what he sees is found in the essay on Baudelaire, *Selected Essays,* p. 344.

"gramophone" makes it also mechanical. The "automatic hand" has already appeared, with a similar implication, in "Rhapsody on a Windy Night." Of course the shift in values is projected by the parody of Goldsmith's song; in that poem, "When lovely woman stoops to folly," her only art is—to die. Both likeness and difference are responsible for the irony.

"This music crept by me upon the waters"—it is a synoptic music, amplifying Ariel's dirge; and the speaker is once more Ferdinand. This music transports him to another music in the haunts of fishmen—he is one too—near the church of Magnus Martyr; the collocation becomes more than geographical, whether in a Biblical or a Fisher King context. What the church holds is "inexplicable," but not unhinted; its colors bear watching in the next section. Here "in Lower Thames Street" he hears the Thames song; now it runs less softly.

The change of verse form provides the transition, but it is not unexpected because of the early distinction between his song and that of the Thames. Of course the notes state this transition to the Song of the Thames-daughters (the departed "nymphs") and further indicate that the three speak in turn from line 292 to 306 inclusive. But without this knowledge little would be missed, since their story is the same story. The two opening stanzas, or the song as distinct from its story, contrast present and past scenes of the river, which are centered in "barge" and "shell." Both craft are marked by "red," but white and gold are absent in the first scene and distributed in the second. In the modern scene Ionic "white and gold" hold an inexplicable splendor in the church, perhaps suggestive of the Grail. And since these are the waters of Babylon, Zion may be suggested by Magnus Martyr. The chorus might be recognized by an opera-goer, but we also have the note. This refrain of the Rhine-daughters in *Götterdämmerung* ("the judgment of the gods") laments the loss of the Rhinegold or beauty of the river; it performs a similar function here, for other guardians of the gold; and again the poem returns to Wagner to express a theme of desolation. Elizabeth and Leicester both figure in Spenser's *Prothalamium* and give continuity to the "affairs" of the river, not to its drift and pollution.

As the Thames-daughters recount their story, we learn that they, like the Rhine-daughters, have been violated. The scene carries them down the river to the sea, and the moral journey is similar, ending in a state that "can connect Nothing with nothing," that calls its violation merely the "broken fingernails" of people who expect nothing. The syncopation of the chorus to that flippant, modern "la la" repeats the last ironic echo of the gramophone.

But "the waters of Leman" flow on; "red sails" still carry the leman, like St. Augustine, to Carthage. The protagonist finishes the song which he has heard, connecting it with meaning, in which it has failed; for Carthage, like Mylae, was familiar to the Phoenician

Sailor, his card. Now the sermon enters the song of the Thames. We can read the "burning" line without becoming aware of Buddha's Fire Sermon, but not without being aware of its theme of passion or lust. And we do not need to know St. Augustine in order to know out of what the Lord plucks—out of this burning, or these waters. It may help to know that St. Augustine said, "I entangle my steps with these outward beauties, but Thou pluckest me out, O Lord, Thou pluckest me out"; or that Buddha preached that moral regeneration begins by "conceiving an aversion" for the lusts of the flesh; but these details merely amplify the significance of "burning" that is already in the poem.

Eliot's notes are interesting for his evaluation of his sources, but they are important chiefly for their emphasis on the collocation of Buddha and St. Augustine. In terms of the poem, theirs is a better wisdom than that of Madame Sosostris, and it is the same for both. The impact which their wisdom loses by reason of poetic economy, it recovers by virtue of its culminating position, which has the whole weight of the lust theme behind it. The syntactic ambiguity of the final "burning" suggests, of course, that burning may define the means by which one is plucked out as well as the state from which one is plucked. As the river's song ends on the theme of being plucked out, we may recall the introduction:

> the last fingers of leaf
> Clutch and sink into the wet bank.

And so they clutch and sink into the waters of Leman
unless they are plucked out.

IV

When "Death by Water is executed in Part IV," it
marks the end of the journey on "the waters of Leman,"
the ultimate fear represented by the "drowned Phoe-
nician Sailor." It rewrites the dirge which associated
Ferdinand with the Sailor, and does so with the con-
clusion that finished a similar sequence of experience
for the old Phoenician waiter in "Dans le Restaurant."
This is the negative issue for such experience. It is
significant that this is the only part without notes—the
earlier note belongs to the second St. Augustine allu-
sion at the end of Part III; here the poet is his own
source, his own explanation.

This part describes the usual way of becoming
free from the fire of passion, not the way of self-dis-
cipline. Here the Sailor is deprived of his lust for the
"outward beauties" and the "profit and loss." Sea cur-
rents pick the lust from his bones, and he reverses the
course of his life as he enters the vortex. There may
be a reminiscence here of the sea-dogs of Scylla and
the whirlpool of Charybdis; or of Virgil's allusion (*Ec-
logue VI*) to Scylla's whirlpool and her sea-hounds that
destroyed sailors. This conclusion now finds it unneces-

sary to say, "it was a painful fate," but necessary to add to the injunction,

> Gentile or Jew
> O you who turn the wheel and look to windward.

And with this addition comes the "Wheel"—of fortune or fate as well as of ships—which appeared in the For- tune. If the epitaph says, with Edmund in *King Lear,*

> The wheel is come full circle; I am here,

it concludes with still more point,

> Consider Phlebas, who was once handsome and tall
> as you.

Hence this part closes, after the fashion of others, by including the audience in its frame of reference.

But if the ultimate fate of the protagonist has been indicated, neither his fortune as told by the Madame, nor his experience in the Hyacinth garden, has been exhausted. Hence what remains must belong to a dif- ferent order of experience from that which properly terminates in death by water, or else to a different attitude toward water.

V

After "Death by Water," representing the fate of his card, the agony of the protagonist is intensified, and he turns from the water that drowns to the water that saves—to the search for another river, associated with the origin of the Tarot cards. Now the gardens and

agony of Part I merge into the trials of Christ or the
Hanged God, and unite them in the conclusion that
he is dead and we are dying. Now "the agony in stony
places" and its fear are intensified both by thirst for
water and doubt of its existence. The search of Part V
—for its parts make one journey—leads ultimately to
the sacred river and its wisdom. Throughout, the il-
lusionary character of the protagonist's vision increases
as his fortune converges.

The experience of agony and its doubt rise out of
the physical conditions of this journey through the
Waste Land, now the desert scene of Part I which
emphasizes the need of water. After observing, "here
is no water but only rock," the spirit is tortured by the
desire of water and no rock, or rock and also water,
or merely the sound of water, even the illusion of its
sound; "but there is no water." This torment has de-
veloped, by thematic imagery, from the "red rock"
through the "Lady of the Rocks" to "only rock."

Physical and spiritual anguish distort his vision as
he walks with the last shadow of his fortune, the Fisher
King, once guardian of the Grail. Beside this unnamed
figure he sees another, "gliding wrapt in a brown man-
tle, hooded"; it is the Hanged Man or Christ. But again
uncertainty besets him, for he cannot identify the fig-
ure. The notes as well as Part I prepare us for "the
journey to Emmaus," and thus help to confirm the
identity of Christ but add little to the essential ex-
perience. This too is a journey made by the "slow of

heart to believe all that the prophets have spoken" (Luke 24), including resurrection; but none of the notes really adds to the realization of its agony.

Likewise, as the vision continues, "the present decay of eastern Europe" is realized quite apart from any need to identify it by a note. It organizes the chaos of the Waste Land, out of earlier materials in the poem, into an unreal image that turns them inside out and upside down. There is "maternal lamentation," as for the dead god; but the "hooded hordes" have their hoods because of their inability to see the "hooded" one. Here we find the "crowds of people, walking round in a ring"—the last item mentioned by Madame Sosostris; they already simulate the motions of Phlebas "entering the whirlpool." Now the unreal city extends to the east, embracing centers of various cultures; the "lady of situations" fiddles lullabies on her hair to "bats with baby faces," adding frustration to maternal lamentation; the bells, towers, and chanting voices of "The Fire Sermon" are all inverted; the "empty cisterns and exhausted wells" dry up the fountain and cistern of the Ecclesiastes passage echoed in Part I, where the poem centers on the "dust" image.

After the vision of the disintegrating city, the protagonist draws near the chapel "in this decayed hole among the mountains"; the reader should recall the mountains of Part I. The chapel, the note as well as the Grail theme tells us, is more than a chapel; it is the Perilous Chapel of the Grail legend, and the Perilous Cemetery is also suggested. But they have lost their terrors, and hence their meaning. The spirit's abode is in ruins, "only the wind's home," and its "dry bones can harm no one"; it belongs to "rats' alley." Here we should recall the opening of Part III: "the wind Crosses the brown land, unheard." The quester denies their former meaning; and then, as with Peter, the cock crows, but as if in a French nursery rhyme. It is another use of the bird sounds that are so significant in the poem, and also of the irony of the naïve. But only a weathercock stood on the rooftree in a flash of lightning—yet it is a herald of light. If this is the storm of the legend, the weathercock on the wind's home serves to point its direction, even to herald the "damp gust bringing rain." In terms of the nature symbolism (vegetation myth) it answers the doubt and denial: there is water, announced in a flash of lightning.

And Ganga (the Ganges) in the Waste Land waits for it. The sacred river, now sunken, was the home of the earliest vegetation myths, and its religious thought is represented here by words from an Upanishad, which is identified in the notes. Then we hear the "reverberation of thunder of spring over distant mountains," which these words interpret. They are the conditions of the promise of spring which answers the doubt and denial expressed in this quest for the water of life.

The onomatopoetic voice of the Thunder is not left untranslated in the poem, for each command is suggested by the response. The question supplies "give" and the answer follows. Their giving has been a surrender to passion, not love—as the poem abundantly illustrates. Yet, while self-regarding, this is their only evidence of life or existence; but it is not found in their obituaries, epitaphs ("memories"), or wills.

The second command is less clearly suggested, but it again is opposite to their reality. The prison of self in which each is locked prevents his sharing the concerns of others. Sympathy would open this prison, which has been locked by pride. Only at nightfall celestial rumors momentarily restore the broken exile of pride.[9] The note quotes a philosophical basis for this isolation of the self, which frustrates the potentiality even of their kind of giving.

The reply to the third command clearly indicates "control," or response to control. This response of the heart counters the surrender to blood and is presented in imagery appropriate to the Sailor and Part IV. It extends that moral from the fate of the Sailor to an image of the heart glad in obedience to the will, from its "blood shaking" to "beating obedient." This completes the conditions of ascent to the higher love which might develop out of their experience, including that of the protagonist, and which would relieve their anguish.[10] These commands have all been violated in the Waste Land.

---

9. In the syntax of this passage the line pauses are heavier than the internal punctuation.

10. See "Dante," *Selected Essays,* pp. 234-35.

If this is the visionary journey which the protagonist takes in search of the water of life, it leaves him sitting upon the shore, with the arid plain rather than the unreal city behind him. Once more fishing, his final guise is that of the Fisher King, to whose line he belongs; but without regeneration his fate is as hopeless as that of the Sailor. Having traveled the Grail road to no avail, he ends in the knowing but helpless state of the Fisher King. Now that the Thunder has spoken, he is the Man with Three Staves—with three cardinal virtues that could be supports, that would insure the rain. But awareness is not will, and so he thinks of preparing for death, with a question that recalls Isaiah (38. 1): "Set thine house in order: for thou shalt die, and not live." This preparation involves some account of his fishing for life, of the fragments or "broken images" which he has shored against his ruins.

These define not only his predicament and state of mind, but the discoveries that are indicated in the poem. As partial quotations they are in fact "fragments" that have their full meaning in other contexts; they summarize the "broken images" of truth left in the Waste Land. Even nursery rhymes may contain or hide terrible truths; so "London Bridge" presents an image of modern disintegration, of sinking into the river. And these fragments follow: "Then he hid him in the fire which refines them . . . when shall I be as the swallow—O swallow swallow . . . the Prince of Acquitaine at the ruined tower." This is the state of

mind that attends the approaching "wrack" of Ferdi-
nand. If the tower points to his ruins, there may be a
saving ambiguity in this salvage. These fragments are
all identified in the notes, but they speak for them-
selves; however, their connections require some com-
ment. The first—from the Arnaut Daniel passage again
—presents an image of voluntary suffering for purga-
tion, the purgatorial burning hinted at the end of Part
III; the second expresses the desire for regeneration,
and connects with the nightingale image of "inviolable
voice"; the third, to which the swallow's attention
seems to be implored, presents an image of the speaker's
predicament, suggesting both the tower of self and the
ruined chapel. Thus, even in their broken state, these
fragments form a pattern.

Then the protagonist turns on the reader, as he
turned at the close of Part I; and declares, in words
of *The Spanish Tragedy* (IV. i), "Why then Ile fit you"
—that is, supply you with what is suitable. And the
irony is capped, while the seriousness is hidden, by the
addition, "Hieronymo's mad againe." We may recall
that the "show" Hieronymo promised was to be his re-
venge; that he could supply it because he had given
his youth to "fruitless poetry"; and that its parts were
originally in "sundry Languages." If these fragments
substitute for the show, their ironic overtones may
echo through these associations—even if the author has
not thought it good, or possible, to set them down in

English, "more largely, for the easier understanding to every public reader." Now the repetition of the Sanskrit commands, supported by the Upanishad ending, sounds like the mad talk of Hieronymo, and hallucinative vision appears to end in madness.

If this account of the poem seems to minimize the anthropological framework, it is for a very simple reason. The framework is a means rather than an end, for the end is concerned with both the development and the decline of religious feeling in modern man. It is true that the anthropology reflects this development in the history of the race, but this reflection lends weight rather than direction to the poem. Neither is its direction taken from the idea that "where the anthropological outlook prevails, sanctions wither." While the emotional significance of the poem at no point is independent of this framework, it is likewise not equivalent to the framework, even when it seems most congruent.

The Hollow Men

To the derivation of this title from a combination of "The Hollow Land" by William Morris and "The Broken Men" by Kipling, Eliot himself has lent countenance.[11] But it is easier to believe that it may have come from Shakespeare's *Julius Caesar* (IV. ii):

---

11. See Geoffrey Tillotson, *Essays in Criticism and Research*, p. 156 n.

> When love begins to sicken and decay,
> It useth an enforced ceremony.
> There are no tricks in plain and simple faith;
> But hollow men, like horses hot at hand,
> Make gallant show and promise of their mettle;
> But when they should endure the bloody spur,
> They fall their crests, and, like deceitful jades,
> Sink in the trial.

If these are not Eliot's "hollow men," they are close enough to raise questions in the mind; and that is the only reason for pursuing the matter.

This poem (1925) is provided with two epigraphs, one pointing to a basic contrast and the other to a basic resemblance. The hollow men are antithetic to "Mistah Kurtz" but like the "Old Guy," that is, the effigy of Guy Fawkes. The hero of Conrad's *Heart of Darkness* enjoys an advantage over the hollow men, not least in the fact that he is dead and they only deadened. Kurtz and Guy Fawkes both were "lost violent souls," not hollow men. But the effigy of Guy Fawkes is a hollow man, for this epigraph derives from the game of make-believe in which children use a stuffed effigy of Guy Fawkes as a means to beg pennies for fireworks on the fifth of November. The relation of this epigraph to the poem, however, suggests another inference: as children make a game of make-believe out of Guy Fawkes so we make a similar game out of religion. The game ritual of the poem supports this implication.

I

The first lines bring the title and epigraph into critical relationship. We are like the Old Guy, effigies stuffed with straw. It may be observed that the first and last parts of this poem indicate a church service, and the ritual of effigies is suggested throughout. The action of this part is indicative of the service: "Leaning together . . . whisper together," the voices "quiet and meaningless" as the service drones on. Then the paradoxes, in which one term denies the other, turn these effigies into abstractions, devoid of even their arid appearance, self-contradictory even in this realm. The erstwhile worshipers disappear in a blur of shape, shade, gesture, to which no reality is attached. Then the crucial orientation is developed, toward "death's other Kingdom." Those who have crossed unafraid remember us—except for the ironic qualification—in terms of the basic opposition between Kurtz and the Old Guy, "not as lost violent souls," but only as the effigies of this service. Now we know where we are in a larger sense, at least that we are in a kingdom of death. And let us observe that the confusing kingdoms of death in the poem are distinguished rather simply: first, the kingdoms of death without relation to God or church have no capital; second, death's real kingdom finds its similitude in life as the "dream" or "twilight" kingdom.

II

Part II defines the hollow men in relation to the reality which those "with direct eyes" have met, and develops the contrast implied by "direct." Fortunately, the eyes he dare not meet even in dreams do not appear in "death's dream kingdom." There they are only reflected, indirect and broken light; wind is reflected by a swinging tree; voices are another illusion of the wind; all is perceived indirectly, and not without beauty. The images are reminiscent of Biblical imagery, but this kingdom resembles Dante's limbo of Trimmers.

He too would be no nearer, but would also wear intentional disguises—those proper to the scarecrow, behaving, like the tree, as the wind behaves. He would be no nearer, no more direct, in this twilight kingdom. He fears the ultimate vision. The eyes in this poem evoke a range of feeling dominated by that which the eyes of Charon excite in Dante (*Inferno*, C. 3).

III

Part III defines this similitude of death's kingdom in relation to the worship of the hollow men. A dead, arid land, like its people, it raises stone images of the spiritual, which are supplicated by the dead. And again the "fading star" establishes a sense of remoteness from reality.

The image of frustrated love which follows is a moment of anguished illumination suspended between the two kingdoms of death. "Waking alone"—not quite out of the dream kingdom—at a propitious time, lips that would adore pray instead to a broken image, for the impulse is frozen. The "broken stone" unites the "stone images" and the "broken column," which bent the sunlight.

IV

Part IV explores this impulse in relation to the land, which now darkens perceptibly as the valley of the shadow of death. Now there are not even similitudes of eyes, and the "fading" becomes the "dying" star. The land as a "hollow valley" carries a ghostly reflection of the human physiognomy in decay, ending as the broken, inarticulate, image of the lost kingdoms of the Old Testament exiles. And with this declination comes the awareness that the indirect meeting found in aspects of beauty must yield to the direct meeting which has been shunned, for this is the last of meeting places.

In action the hollow men now "grope together And avoid speech," gathered on the banks of the swollen river which must be crossed to "death's other kingdom." The contrast with Part I is clear, and the river suggests that of Dante's *Inferno* (C. 3).

Without any eyes at all they are without any vision,

unless "the eyes" return as the "perpetual," not a fad-
ing or dying, star; as the "multifoliate rose" of this
kingdom. But for empty men this is only a hope. As
star becomes rose, so the rose becomes the rose window
of the church; the rose as an image of the church, and
multifoliate, appears in Dante's *Paradiso* (C. 31-32).

V

But Part V develops the reality, not the hope, of
empty men; the cactus, not the rose. And it begins with
the prickly pear ritual of cactus land; the nursery level
of make-believe mocks the hope of empty men. In de-
sire they "circumambulate" the pear, but are frustrated
by the prickles. Here we may recall "the hour when
we are Trembling with tenderness," for the poem now
develops that frustration of impulse. At various levels,
in various aspects of life, between the impulse and its
realization there falls the frustrating shadow of fear,
the essential shadow of this land. Yet the Shadow is
more than fear: it concentrates the valley of the shadow
into a shape of horror, almost a personification of its
negative character. The antiphonal division of this
part, marked by the type, exhibits the irony which leads
"round the mulberry bush" to the last line.

Various stages are interrupted by the interpolation
of elements that qualify this thwarting Shadow: after
the first, the passage from the Lord's Prayer relates
the Shadow to religion, with irony in the attribution;

after the second, the response about the length of life relates it to the burden of life; and after the third, the Lord's Prayer again relates it to the Kingdom that is so hard. This repetition follows the thwarting of the series that produces life itself, frustrating the essence from descent to being (see *Purgatorio*, 31: 107). This is the essential irony of their thwarted lives.

Then the rather ambiguous relation of these interrupting elements to the Shadow is made more explicit. This is done by turning these responses, minus their predicate complements, into the main chant, with the result that each completion hesitates between its former complement and the Shadow, and at the same time suggests by its truncation the final interruption. This end comes by way of ironic completion as the nursery rhyme again takes up its repetitive round ("This is the way we go to church"), and terminates with the line that characterizes the equivocating excuses. They are the whimpers of fear with which the hollow men end, neither the bang of Guy Fawkes Day nor of the "lost violent soul." The conclusion also transforms the liturgical "world without end."

In Part V the frustration of reality is described by the abstractions introduced in Part I; life is frustrated at every level, and this accounts for the nature of the land and the character of its people. By placing God in a causal relation to this condition, the poem develops an irony which results in the "whimper." But the most devastating irony is formal: the extension of game ritual into liturgical form.

The "Shadow" derives from Dowson's most famous poem, "Non sum qualis eram bonae sub regno Cynarae." [12] Of course it has been transformed, but it is still qualified by the memory. The part to which it most obviously connects earlier in the poem appears in the "lips that would kiss"; the desire that is frustrated there preserves this ambiguity in Part V. Other repetitions in Dowson's poem besides the shadow of Cynara have probably had some effect on Eliot's poem. In Dowson, after each lapse in faith, which is followed by the line "And I was desolate and sick of an old passion," there is a statement of its effect, followed by his declaration of faith. After each lapse, the shadow precipitates these consequences, and this circumstance may have suggested Eliot's transformation. Some of Dowson's other lines may lurk behind some of Eliot's: possibly the causal line, "Yea, all the time, because the dance was long"; perhaps "I have been faithful to thee, Cynara!" has become "For Thine is the Kingdom."

Comparison suggests that Eliot's theme of the frustration of desire by fear still carries oppositions and overtones of the poem from which its "shadow" is derived. And this frustration is finally the reason why the eyes are obscured and the land a realm of shadows. Here Eliot, to use his words on Baudelaire, is "looking

---

12. This was conjectured by Geoffrey Tillotson and confirmed by Eliot; see G. Tillotson, *Essays in Criticism and Research,* p. 156 n.

into the Shadow." Thus Dowson's poem provided the hint by which Part V amalgamated all the others, translating the lack of substance which they described into the thwarting shadow. One reason for considering the possible genesis of Part V is the light it throws on Eliot's piecemeal mode of composition, which will be discussed later.

Chapter **6**

ARIEL POEMS
AND ASH-WEDNESDAY

The Ariel Poems, named for the series in which they appeared, were published between 1927 and 1930; only "Marina" appeared after the publication of *Ash-Wednesday*. They all explore new experience, or extend an experience already begun. It pays to notice the subjects that are now significant to Eliot: in the Bible, the story of the Magi, the story of Simeon; in Dante, the deflection of the will from God; in Shakespeare, the recovery of Marina. They make another story in themselves, which Donne might have called a progress of the soul. But individually they are also contemporary. The "Journey of the Magi," for example, is not a piece of antiquarianism, a recreation of Biblical story, but, as usual in Eliot's use of history, something that continues to happen.

Of course there is much to consider in their exploration of new possibilities in syntax, rhythm, rhyme, diction and imagery; in imagery, especially that of nature touched by Biblical use; in phrasing also the influence of Biblical poetry, especially its balance. All of it belongs to a search for a new form for a new content; and it is true in effect, if not in fact, to say that *Ash-Wednesday* is composed of Ariel poems that united to form a whole.

Journey of the Magi

In "Journey of the Magi" (1927), now clipt in its elliptical syntax, now swinging into a looser rhythm, but never indulging in rhyme, one of the Magi recounts the journey to Christ (Matthew 2) long after the event and ponders its consequences. They went to a birth, but their rebirth was a death to the old life. He would do it again; but now, alien among his own people, he would be glad to die. The description of the journey—in nature from death to life—not only projects the inner struggle of the Magi, but foreshadows events to come in the life of Christ; especially his crucifixion, suggesting by three trees in a western scene the Death implicit in the Birth. Symbolic extension pervades the poem; see the white horse in Revelation (6:2 or 19:11).

This part of the poem illustrates an aspect of Eliot's theory of poetic composition for which he has provided the necessary data. In *The Use of Poetry and the Use of Criticism* he asks,

Why, for all of us, out of all that we have heard, seen, felt, in a lifetime, do certain images recur, charged with emotion, rather than others? The song of one bird, the leap of one fish, at a particular place and time, the scent of one flower, an old woman on a German mountain path, six ruffians seen through an open window playing cards at night at a small French railway junction where there was a water-mill . . . (p. 141)

The water-mill and the six ruffians can be recognized in this part, but they have been given a new context in Gospel story which uses them in an intelligible way while they in turn qualify that context with other associations. And such associations are the very elements which make this event continue to happen. Let the reader note any persistent bird, flower, or other symbol in Eliot's poetry.

The passage from Lancelot Andrewes with which the poem begins may be located in his essay on Andrewes, but the emotional context is not to be found in Andrewes. In general the passages which attract Eliot as poet are those which attract him as critic, and are therefore very often cited in his criticism. This poem centers in the ambiguity of "Birth or Death," and derives its peculiar quality from the contrast between its matter-of-fact account and the extraordinary effect of the journey; its tone is that of understatement, "it was (you may say) satisfactory." But its emotional effect culminates in the mixed feelings of the Magus; their death, too, had been foreshadowed and required; and "another death" now suggests escape rather than consummation.

A Song for Simeon

For "A Song for Simeon" (1928) the story of Simeon (Luke 2:25-35) should be read in order to see how Eliot has renewed and reinterpreted the story, which includes this petition: "Lord, now lettest thou thy servant depart in peace, according to thy word." Central to this interpretation as well as to the development of the poem is the iteration and change in Simeon's petition as he, "waiting for the consolation of Israel," foresees the consequences of the coming of the Lord's Christ.

The poem begins with the ambiguous "birth season of decease," when Roman hyacinths, indicative of the foreign domination, bloom in bowls amidst the dead season and Simeon waits for death. After he prays "Grant us thy peace"—for he has been a good and faithful servant—he shudders to think what will happen "When the time of sorrow is come," when their consolation comes to death (Luke 23). Before that time, he iterates, before the "stations" and "sorrow" of Calvary, "Grant us thy peace," let the Christ child "grant Israel's consolation" to an old man without a future; it is thy word. While "they shall praise Thee and suffer" for it in every generation, that is not for me, "Not for me the ultimate vision." Now the petition is wholly personal, "Grant me thy peace"; and its character is emphasized by the parenthesis on the martyrdom of

Christ, pointing the self-sacrifice of God. The last lines
extend the Simeon state of mind into the future: the
fatigue of his life is like that of those after him; his dy-
ing is like that of those after him. And the final petition
asks that the faithful servant, satisfied with "having
seen thy salvation," be allowed to depart—without
further participation. The "saints' stair" is not for
Simeon.

Animula

"Animula" (1929), a little soul suggested less by
Hadrian than by Dante (*Purgatorio* 16:85-93), "issues
from the hand of God, the simple soul," to the world
of time or experience. Responsive with potential vir-
tues, the simple soul begins its adulteration. It pursues
the good with pleasure until checked by imperatives
that only subvert its impulses. Ready to confound "the
actual and the fanciful," the growing soul proves an
easy victim to "the drug of dreams" when the actual
becomes "the pain of living"; and encyclopaedic in-
formation is its final retreat from life. It learns to dis-
trust rather than to discriminate and control.

Thus it issues from the hand of time with all the
faults that deaden the soul; to live again only in the
silence after the last Eucharist. "For," as Eliot said in
The Sacred Wood, "in Dante's Hell souls are not dead-
ened, as they mostly are in life." Hence the injunction
to pray for these products of time, these misshapen

souls, destroying themselves in various forms of violence. These characters, ending with the modern Adonis or Actaeon, show that unless the will learns moral allegiance the child is indeed father to the man. To "pray for us now and at the hour of our birth" is thus to pray for deadened souls that live only when made to face reality. It is another turn on the paradox of the Magus, "Birth or Death?" The nice evolution of thought in this sad poem may be instanced by the meaning of Christmas first and last, or of "running stags" in the final chase.

Ash-Wednesday

Parts of *Ash-Wednesday* were published separately: Part II appeared in 1927, Part I in 1928, and Part III in 1929. The poem appeared as a whole in April of 1930. Dante has become a more pervasive influence, speaking now to an Anglo-Catholic. The title associates the poem with a day of commination and humility, and the poem itself suggests the Mass at many points. In the ritual for Ash-Wednesday the priest, dipping his thumb in ashes, marks the sign of the cross on the forehead while he intones: "Remember, man, that thou art dust, and unto dust thou shalt return." This reminds us of the exile from the Garden of Eden (Genesis, 3). Hence the need of man to turn from the world to God. This provides the basic turning theme of the poem and implies the complementary theme.

Both themes are associated with the title under which Part I was first published and which survives in the initial motif. It was "Perch'Io Non Spero," which comes from the poem by Cavalcanti that Rossetti translated as "Ballata, written in Exile at Sarzana." This poem expresses devotion to his lady as death approaches. In the translation it begins,

> Because I think not ever to return,
> Ballad, to Tuscany . . .

It gives the initial theme, the first line, and relates it, as Rossetti's title indicates, to exile. The chief reason for citing this source is to illustrate the combination of the turning theme and the exile theme rather than the way in which Eliot's mind combines scattered materials in a basic theme. Of course this poem is related to his source in the *Vita Nuova*. If we keep alert to the things between which the speaker turns, we shall have less trouble in following the poem and may even perceive a development. We should remember that the basic opposites for Ash-Wednesday are the world and God, or the desert and garden.

Ash-Wednesday draws inspiration, both generally and particularly, from the closing cantos of the *Purgatorio* dealing with the Earthly Paradise. On their relation to the *Vita Nuova* consult Eliot's treatment of both in his *Dante;* no guide could be more fundamental. To these cantos must be added the Scripture on which Dante draws, notably the Song of Solomon,

Ezekiel, and the Revelation of St. John, which may
have influenced the mode of vision. Comparison with
The Waste Land will also prove instructive in many
ways; woman, for example, now becomes the symbol
of a more beneficent love, "the attraction towards God."
On this change and its visionary form the *Vita Nuova*
becomes relevant with section XVIII.

I

In developing the turning theme the poet first states
why he does not hope to turn again to the world; hav-
ing lost his ambition or force, he abandons the struggle.
The "agéd eagle" may derive point from Psalm 103:5,
"Who satisfieth thy mouth with good things; so that
thy youth is renewed like the eagle's"; or from Isaiah
40:31, "But they that wait upon the Lord shall renew
their strength; they shall mount up with wings as
eagles." But why should he regret the usual loss of
power? Then, with mounting certainty, he declares that
he will never know the "positive hour" again or the one
real though transitory power, because he cannot drink
in its source. For the moment the power remains enig-
matic and the source appears to be merely nature, but
his failure leads to a spiritual consequence and the
imagery subsequently develops meaning as the Garden.

The reason for this lack of hope is then given: things
are always limited by time and place, and these have
passed for him. Hence he rejoices in accepting his lot,

at least in this certainty; he resigns himself to renounce the blesséd face and voice associated with religion. Having found nothing in either opposite to which he could turn, he must begin at the bottom, without hope, "to construct something Upon which to rejoice." But he also prays for mercy and for forgetfulness of the matters which he has been discussing. This admission will have to answer for him—he would give up the struggle—"May the judgment not be too heavy."

It should be observed that he has now extended the situation beyond himself. And some extenuation is then advanced. The wings of the eagle—aged because of the state of mind—are now merely fans to beat the air; but, though he is unable to fly, the difficulty is less in the will than in the power and present air. Therefore, he petitions, teach us both to care and not to care— depending on the object; teach us patience in waiting for death—the object of his final prayer, taken from the *Ave Maria*. And death, the reminder of Ash-Wednesday, provides the transition to Part II, which also develops the salutation of the prayer. The introduction of liturgical themes is likewise found in the closing cantos of the *Purgatorio*.

In Part I, largely because of doubt, the springs of action are dried up; hence the speaker, having no hope, can turn neither to the world nor to God. In possible states of mind it represents the nadir of despair. Having renounced both the world and the hope of salva-

tion, he goes on in Part II to construct out of death
something upon which to rejoice.

II

Part II was published under the title and epigraph
of "Salutation, *e vo significando*." The nature of the
salutation of this Lady is indicated by the epigraph,
which derives from the *Purgatorio* (24:53-54): "I am
one who, when Love inspires me take note, *and go
setting it forth* after the fashion which he dictates
within me." For knowledge of the "Ladies that have
intelligence of Love" see the context of this passage
and the *Vita Nuova* (XIX). Although these passages
are not required in order to read the poem, they pre-
pare us for the possible origin and development of this
intelligence of love. And the epigraph alone suggests
something to which he can turn that is more positive
than death. It should be observed that the symbols in
Ash-Wednesday are often generic, presenting various
aspects in different contexts, and their ambiguity begins
with garden, blesséd face and voice, and Lady. The
face and voice, for example, relate to incarnations of
love, first seen in the Lady; and the rose of love is re-
lated to the yew of grief. But we may wonder how the
death theme can be developed by setting forth an
inspiration of love.

The opening lines suggest Elijah (1 Kings 19) when,
having been threatened with death by Jezebel, he sat

down under a juniper tree and prayed that he might die. The leopards no doubt are appropriate to the desert, but they are more than a substitute for rats as images of destruction; they represent the attraction of death, not the horror but the peace of dissolution. As in Dante (*Inferno* I) they are agents of destruction but salutary. Here they have fed on the organs to which the lusts of life are related, and by their color assume the aspect of a purifying release. This vision resembles that of Ezekiel (37); hence the words of Ezekiel help to develop its significance, first by the question, in which the "voice" of Part I is heard. But the answer of the bones (or desire in them) is not that of Ezekiel: "behold, they say, Our bones are dried, and our hope is lost: we are cut off for our parts." These bones owe their clean brightness to a Lady who "honours the Virgin in meditation" and inspires them; in this cleansing by white agents for a white cause the self "here dissembled" surrenders his pride and offers his love to the posterity of the land he knows, the desert. This act "recovers" the unconsumed parts, those rejected by the destroyers. And the bones, now white like the Lady, imitate her devotion, "atone to forgetfulness," for which he merely prayed in Part I. Self-abnegation is an advance over his previous state, in which he suffered the frustration of self.

But the words of Ezekiel introduce an irony into the answer that "there is no life" in the bones: "prophesy to the wind," for only it will listen. Although there is no hope in them, only the wind will hear their prophecy. And the bones prophesy in song, with the chirping of the grasshopper or the burden of desire in Ecclesiastes (12:5): "and the grasshopper shall be a burden and desire shall fail: because man goeth to his long home." The litany of the bones offers their salutation to the Lady of paradoxes who is now the Garden which reconciles all paradoxes. To distinguish this Rose from another white rose we may recall the prayer to the Virgin in the *Paradiso* (33:7-9): "In thy womb was lit again the love under whose warmth in the eternal peace this flower hath thus unfolded." The "single Rose," dedicated to the Virgin, personifies devotion; she "Is now the Garden Where all loves end," now the divine "Speech without word and Word of no speech"; and is therefore invoked to give thanks to the Virgin "For the Garden Where all love ends"—as Dante found. The "single Rose" may image the ultimate flower and be the interpreter of the Earthly Paradise to man. This Lady, who incarnates the love of the Virgin and so qualifies the speaker's, is the first incarnation of love in the poem and leads to the Garden where he could not drink.

In death the bones now rejoice in the division of the parts which had tormented the speaker in Part I. Again the words of Ezekiel (45:1) are heard in altered form: "Moreover, when ye shall divide by lot the land for inheritance, ye shall offer an oblation unto the Lord, an holy portion of the Land." If this portion is the Garden, the land the bones shall divide is the desert, and in death "neither division nor unity matters." They have their inheritance, dissolution, "the blessing of sand," cessation of the war of the members. In this atonement to forgetfulness of self, his love has been offered to the posterity of his desert and his thanks to the "Ladies that have intelligence of Love"; but the Garden is not seen as the long home of his bones. Yet he has begun "to construct something," to pass beyond despair; and for the spirit in his bones a potentiality in the death of the members beyond its peace has emerged. In death he has seen not the greatest threat to the self and its lusts, but release from them; in the love which this death reveals he has found both the cause and form of triumph over self.

III

Part III was first published under the title of *Som de l'Escalina*, "the summit of the stairway," which derives from the famous Provençal speech of Arnaut Daniel (*Purgatorio* 26: 146) that is used again in the next part. In fact, it may be said to have been present already in the Lady, for this is the last stanza: "Now I pray you, by that Goodness which guideth you to the summit of the stairway, be mindful in due time of my pain." But this title, which points to the Earthly Paradise, does not mean that we can impose Dante's stairway on Eliot's poem, only that we have something comparable; indeed, ascent is the mode of realizing the higher love in *Ash-Wednesday*.

"At the first turning of the second stair" he has already passed one stage in his ascent; the first stair is found in Part II. The "same shape" is one he knows, whose "struggling with the devil of the stairs" he has now passed. This shape is himself, who for the time being has conquered false hopes and fears or the spectre of doubt, which at best is always just behind him. For the clearest illumination of Eliot's type of religious mind read his essay on Pascal, where he speaks of "the demon of doubt which is inseparable from the spirit of belief."

Then he passes through the trial of despair, "dark, damp, jaggéd," suggesting age and decay; remember "the agéd eagle." The third stair brings the trial of hope with its imagery of youth and spring, its suggestion of carnal love, its deceptive appearance of the Garden. Here the appeals to the senses are enticing, not repulsive as in the image of despair. Vision is suddenly released by the window, no longer confined by the darkness; but the appeals to the senses, though broadened, are remote, not immediate as before. The imagery of hope and despair, which emphasizes sensuous appeal or its opposite, points to the loss which constitutes the trial. This centers in the figure of Pan and suggests a pastoral scene rather than the Garden of Part II.

As these "stops and steps of the mind" fade, we

realize that this part, which is also a vision, has now brought us to a "strength beyond hope and despair," to the point where he can utter the concluding petition. In the original prayer this supplication is followed by the words "And my soul shall be healed." Will the sequence be similar here? At least we can say that from the possible hope in death the speaker has gone on to the conquest of hope and despair, to a strength beyond either (see Matthew 8:8). Now "to care and not to care" have grown in meaning, and the highest incarnation of love has been addressed, in humility and emergent faith.

IV

Part IV opens with a syntax that is purposefully vague. Gradually the Lady in white melts into the Mother of the Garden before we come to the petition directed to her, "Sovegna vos"—Arnaut's petition to "be mindful." Now to her color and intelligence of love she has added Mary's color and knowledge of eternal sorrow. As a human being she is partially aware of the divine, paradoxically both ignorant and aware of eternal sorrow; she is both the "bléssed sister" of man and the holy mother. First she walked in the garden between dawn and evening, concerned with trivial things, and "then made strong the fountains and made fresh the springs"—where the speaker could not drink in Part I. In alleviating the desert her actions may characterize either the Lady or the Virgin. She was saluted as the Garden in Part II; now she is petitioned. In this part the appearances of the garden in Part II and Part III are also mingled, thus developing its earlier paradoxes. If "all loves end" in the garden of the Lady, "all love ends" in the Garden of the Virgin. When the colors of Pan are followed by those of Mary, she is also associated with green, but with a deeper significance in the garden.

"Here are the years that walk between" the violet hours of the speaker's life rather than of day; between the two gardens, "bearing away the fiddles and the flutes" seen in Part III, restoring in dreams the lady seen in Part II, the white rose of devotion. Sheathed in the white light of illumination, she restores the past through a grief of reflected brightness; restores the ancient rhyme of love with a new verse rhyming "redeem" with "dream." The new theme is to redeem "the unread vision in the higher dream" while its pageantry of death passes by. The Lady has been associated with white leopards and the "Word of no speech"; now "jewelled unicorns," belonging to the legend of the Virgin, add mystery to the funeral of the Word. This vision is an image like the pageantry that Eliot calls the "high dream" in Dante; here the hearse contains the supreme token of love, of the word now unread.[1]

_____

1. This image may have been suggested by some example of medieval symbolism in which Christ as a unicorn is drawing the ark of the cove-

The silent sister, now veiled like Beatrice but identified by her silence and colors, confirms the meaning of the hearse when she bows and makes the sign of the cross.[2] She is seen from a significant point of view, rather as the sister than as the Mother of Sorrows. And it should be noticed that she stands "between the yews" of mortality and mourning; "behind the garden god" of Part III, whose flute is now breathless. She "bent her head and signed but spoke no word," now "in knowledge of eternal dolour." Though she spoke no word, the fountain again is made strong; and the bird, replacing the flute, sings "redeem the dream," the sign of the word unheard—"unspoken Till the wind shake a thousand whispers from the yew" of mortality. These whispers mean responses, not the rustling of the bones in Ezekiel; but the wind now suggests the restoring breath. The silence must first be broken by the voices of the yew, which now, like the flute, is breathless.

Thus the silent sister has become mindful in due time of his pain because he has uttered the theme of redemption. The yew—associated with the church—is a generic symbol of the eternal sorrow which embraces man and Christ. "And after this our exile" comes from

nant. Perhaps it is worth remarking that for some time in Eliot the Dido myth is suggested by a persistent undertone: beginning in *La Figlia Che Piange* with "O quam te memorem virgo," it passes through the "laquearia" of *The Waste Land* and emerges again in the "ancient rhyme," which recalls Dante's "antico amor" and "antica fiamma" as they recall Virgil's "Agnosco veteris vestigia flammae."

2. The Lady, like Beatrice, melts into the mediator.

the prayer *Salve Regina,* which continues thus: "show unto us the blesséd fruit of thy womb, Jesus." It will be noticed that Eliot leaves this fragment unclosed; it is the only unstopped part of *Ash-Wednesday,* for the revelation follows. But it stands as a broken petition, hesitating, as if fearful, to complete itself. Thus from the conquest of hope and despair he has passed through growing faith to a vision of regeneration, which remains conditional and depends upon the fruit of Mary.

V

Part V deals with the revelation of the Word in the present world. "If the lost word is lost . . ." characterizes the present state of the word of God, but concludes by affirming the presence both of the Word as the manifestation of God and of the word as the revelation of God. The state of the word of God depends upon man, but not his manifestation as the Word. If the Incarnate Word is without a word, both are still "within The world and for the world." But if the Word is for the world, the world is against the Word. The Word was manifested when "the light shone in darkness," and the world still whirled both against and about the Word as its center. "Unstilled" is both a contrast to "silent" and a parallel to "whirled." [3]

---

3. For a vision of the wheel, Eliot's most comprehensive symbol, see Plato's *Republic* (X) or *Timaeus.*

There follows the word of the Word from Micah 6:3, expressing the for and against theme. This question is followed by an answer.

"Where shall the word be found" or heard? Nowhere, for "there is not enough silence." For the walkers in darkness both day and night, there is neither time nor place; for in darkness they "avoid the face" and in noise "deny the voice." This passage recalls the speaker's state in Part I.

Now we turn to the "veiled sister" of the last part. Will she pray for such? These are characterized by all the opposites that led them both to choose and to oppose the Word. Will she pray for those who, like children at the gate, "will not go away and cannot pray"? It should be remembered that the silent sister in Part IV "signed but spoke no word." Although God's word is heard on various occasions, the silence of the agents of divine love in *Ash-Wednesday* is marked.

The opposition is now intensified by a repetition of the question of the Word, which in Micah continues thus: "and wherein have I wearied thee? testify against me."

And the anguish of the speaker increases. "Will the veiled sister" between the trees of "eternal dolour" pray "for those who offend her"? Now their state is more sharply defined; they "are terrified and cannot surrender"; hence they affirm in public and deny in private, even to the end of their hard road, where its rocks are of Mary's color. This conflict puts "the des-

ert in the garden the garden in the desert," and cul-
minates in "spitting from the mouth the withered
appleseed"—the last vestige of their knowledge of
good and evil, which is too agonizing.

The final exclamation of the Word is both a sharp
reminder and an affirmation of his disposition toward
man. Thus the world exiles us from the Word, though
the world turns upon the Word; and man is tortured
on the rack of this antithesis. The word is here, though
the world is against it, and man both for and against;
his will is too weak to realize faith. But the speaker has
now asserted the dire need for grace, confirmed the
presence of the highest love, and expressed the most
agonized concern for his dilemma.

VI

After this extreme development of the difficulty of
turning to God, the poem returns to its initial theme,
but with an altered relation to his turning. In passing
from "because" to "although," the lack of hope passes
from a causal relation to will to a concessive relation to
will; and the significance of this change, which is con-
ducive to grace, is first developed, as in Part I, in rela-
tion to the world.

Although he does not hope, does not wish, to turn to
the world, the appeal of the world returns to him; hence
the interpolated petition of the confessor. Now a wide
window (compare Part III) reveals the beauty of the

world: "unbroken wings" contrast with the "vans" of
Part I, the "lost heart" rejoices again in its lost delights,
the "weak spirit quickens to rebel" for the lust of the
senses, and the "blind eye" once more creates its illu-
sions. In short, the lusts of nature are renewed, where
he appeared to find nothing in Part I.

This is the time between death to the world and birth
to God, the place where three dreams (Lady, Virgin,
Christ) cross between the rocks. "But when the voices
shaken from the yew-tree" of Part IV drift away, let the
other yew of sorrow "be shaken and reply." The lines
are reminiscent of "Gerontion": "These tears are shaken
from the wrath-bearing tree." The yew is the sorrow-
bearing tree. It should be noticed that the "time of ten-
sion" differs from the "brief transit" of life by reversing
"birth and dying"; and that the "dreamcrossed twilight"
relates, not to the "dreams," but to the "empty forms"
that issue from the gate of false dreams in Virgil's
Aeneid (VI). Notice the iteration of "cross" in this
necessary distinction.

Then the speaker invokes both the sanctified sister
and the holy mother to "suffer us not to mock ourselves"
with empty forms, and to teach us the lessons requested
in Part I, with the significant addition of finding "Our
peace in His will"—the great lesson of Dante. Peace is
not to be found in death. And finally, "even among
these rocks" he asks not to be separated from the river
and sea, and then more straightforwardly directs his
petition to God. Added to sister and mother, "spirit of

the river, spirit of the sea," do not augment fountain and garden, but refer obliquely to God (see *Purgatorio* 28:121-26 and *Paradiso* 3:85-87). The last allusion—to God's will as "that sea to which all moves that it createth and that nature maketh"—gives the ultimate resolution to the paradoxes of the changing Lady who leads him to this conclusion. These images, it should be remarked, are some of the images of *Ash-Wednesday* that are explored more significantly in *Four Quartets*.

The reversal is now complete: where he could turn neither to the world nor to God, now although he can turn to the world he desires to turn to God. Indeed, his situation is critical in another way. Although he does "not wish to wish" for worldly things, he does; but his will is not to be separated from God. The return of will toward one strengthens the will toward the other. The contrast of Parts I and VI sets in sharp relief the change of will which is the significant development of the poem. For the poem describes stages of despair, self-abnegation, moral recovery, resurgent faith, need of grace, and renewal of will toward both world and God. Part VI is not a paradox, but a revelation of the basic weakness of his despair in Part I. The exile theme and its complementary turning are now based on greater moral insight and a renewed sense of direction. Emotionally *Ash-Wednesday* develops his experience of love in relation to its various incarnations, marked by an ascent from lower to higher. Intellectually the poem may be understood as a reflection of his remark on Pascal that "his despair, his disillusion, are . . . essential moments in the progress of the intellectual soul; and for the type of Pascal they are the analogue of the drought, the dark night, which is an essential stage in the progress of the Christian mystic." The negative way of the mystic is not the way for the intellectual soul.

Marina

Marina, the lost daughter, derives from Shakespeare's *Pericles;* but for this poem (September 1930) the recovery theme takes on another significance as an image of new life related to the sea, where Marina was born and lost. By the epigraph this vision is related to a somber orientation theme, that of the awakening in Seneca's *Hercules Furens* (1. 1138): "What place is this? What region, what quarter of the world?" The situation is this: Hercules, under a spell of madness brought on him by Juno, kills his family; after the deed he falls into a deep slumber; then he awakens in his right mind and tries to place himself. This is followed by a gradual realization of horror as he discovers his crimes. In Eliot's poem the horror of Seneca fades as the vision of Marina comes, but in the basic orientation theme they complement one another. The vision of Marina is a "grace dissolved in place" that makes unsubstantial the elements of horror, which mean death as she means life. Hence the locating questions in the beginning and ending, and their inclusion of menace as well as relief to a befogged ship.

The poem begins by asking "What images return" to you? Her location is not so much geographical as psychological, a state of mind; she is to be located and known by the images that come back to her. Of course the "daughter" is a personification of hope or potentiality.

For him some sharp images have become unsubstantial. They are images of the lusts or passions known as the seven deadly sins; in particular, the "tooth" of gluttony, the "glory" of pride, the "stye" of sloth, and the "ecstasy" of lust. Of course they all mean spiritual death, and are therefore powerful images.

But all these are now abated by more intangible images, which produce a sense of grace out of some of the locating images, truly "dissolved in place" by the remarkable fusion of "woodsong fog."

Then this perception of grace is translated into images that relate the daughter to the speaker in a vision which is also dissolved as if in water or sleep, or related to fog and lapping water. The face, the pulse, ebbing and flooding, are they given or lent? They seem more remote than the stars and "nearer than the eye"— subjective; like whispers and infant laughter made by hurrying feet among leaves, in sleep "where all the waters meet," and one does not have to ask "What water?"

Then, as if awakening from a dream, his memory

gradually and with difficulty recognizes the "bow," the boat he made long ago, while "unknowing, half conscious, unknown." Thus the focus of his vision shifts, and he realizes that his ship is now barely seaworthy. The next lines bring the consequence of his recovery and awakening. Let him resign his life for this vaguely perceived form, face, and life, which extends to a world of time beyond him. The imagery of realization recalls the imagery of perception in its potential awakening and brings the hope of "new ships."

Now the locating images come back in altered form, the shores related to his ship, the "woodthrush calling," not "singing through the fog." If there is still fog and danger ahead, there is also hope, even guidance. There is a peculiar beauty in "this grace dissolved in place," but the lapping water will acquire a more plangent note in *Four Quartets*.

Chapter 7

UNFINISHED
AND MINOR POEMS

The poems included under this caption, where I place the *Choruses from "The Rock,"* present fewer problems in reading, but more obvious problems in composition. The poems that are called unfinished raise several questions of some concern to the reader of Eliot. On one side they are questions of genesis; on the other, of the relation of parts to wholes. Of particular concern to the reader is the fact that some poems, though separately published, are regarded as unfinished because they are essentially parts rather than wholes. Other aspects relate these parts in form or content to completed poems. While the unfinished poems require some particular comment, we shall first consider the general problem which they present.

"The Hollow Men" was the first poem to illustrate the piecemeal composition and publication that have marked Eliot's longer poems since *The Waste Land.* Only Part V was not published separately, and Part III appeared as the third item in another grouping besides the one found in this poem. It was called "Doris's Dream Songs," [1] and the other two items now make the first two poems under *Minor Poems*. Thus the significant third part once belonged to the dreams of Doris, the companion of Sweeney, and the change points to a later conception. Hence it is that the previously unpublished part of a new poem usually reveals most clearly its principle of unity or transmutation, being the part most immediate to the new or resolving motive of synthesis. Some negative evidence of this practice remains: incomplete sequences, for which the completing parts never came; or rejected parts, for which no sequence was ever found. This practice seems to be an extension of his theory of the poetic mind as "constantly amalgamating disparate experience . . . in the mind of the poet these experiences are always forming new wholes." The same thing evidently happens at a later stage: units apparently complete in themselves unite with other units to form a new whole. The result is that what are published as separate poems may appear later as parts of another poem. Hence the parts that are not published until the new composition appears commonly afford the best insight into the character of such poems.

---

1. See *The Chapbook: A Miscellany,* edited by Harold Monro; No. 39 (1924), pp. 36-37.

Sweeney Agonistes

Sweeney Agonistes appeared in 1932, but its two fragments had been published in 1926 and 1927. Aristophanic melodrama involving the Eumenides is a conception still unrealized in Eliot's plays, for another mood qualifies *The Family Reunion*.[2] It is, however, a direction once proper to his poetry, and not unrealized in it. The union of Aristophanes and music-hall verse is certainly less incongruous than the union of Aristophanes with the Eumenides, and yet Eliot often employs this type of shocking incongruity. It is found in this title, and in the connection the reader is likely to make with Milton. It appears in his irony of the nursery rhyme, or the jarring juxtaposition of terms that belong to the sublime and the ridiculous, in the elements that are sometimes thought to border on, or fall into, caricature.

Perhaps we come closest to his conception of *Sweeney Agonistes* in what he has to say about certain plays of Marlowe and Jonson. He sees in Marlowe's *Jew of Malta*—a play he has used for epigraphs—a kind

---

2. But elements, even rhythms, of *Sweeney Agonistes* persist in the design of *The Cocktail Party* as the drawing-room transforms another Greek story—not of Orestes but of Alcestis. Mr. Francis Fergusson has suggested that the basic pattern which determines plot and character in Eliot's morality plays conforms to the three discontinuous orders of Pascal—"the order of nature, the order of mind, and the order of charity"—about which, Eliot remarked, "the modern world would do well to think." The same distinctions may be found in his poetry.

of savage farce or grim caricature, achieved in a newer "style which secures its emphasis by always hesitating on the edge of caricature at the right moment." [3] In Jonson he finds a similar art of caricature in his simplification of detail and his "flat distortion in the drawing." Jonson's "satire," since it creates its object, "is merely a medium for the essential emotion . . . only incidentally a criticism upon the actual world." [4] Likewise, Eliot's satire is a distortion that derives its meaning less from any direct reflection of the actual world than from its projection of the essential feeling of the author.

One is tempted to see in this play "the Agon of the Fertility Spirit," which enabled Miss Weston to include Greek drama in *From Ritual to Romance* (p. 99). It would be caricature indeed if Sweeney were a Fertility spirit pursued by the "hoo-ha's" of the Eumenides and dedicated to the moral, "Hence the soul cannot be possessed of the divine union, until it has divested itself of the love of created beings." Since this epigraph obviously anticipates *Four Quartets*, the suggested mixture is sufficiently ironic to lift a music-hall libretto into a disturbing atmosphere. But its serious import was concealed by the original title, *Wanna Go Home, Baby?*

---

3. *Selected Essays*, p. 105. See also *The Use of Poetry*, pp. 146-47.
4. *Ibid.*, p. 131.

Fragment of a Prologue

The play is, however, an extension of his achievement in the second part of *The Waste Land,* adapting the vulgar speech and neurasthenic atmosphere to the unctuous superstition of a prostitute world. *Sweeney Agonistes* develops the "good time" theme of the sexual "Game of Chess" into another dimension. In a week-end party at Miss Dorrance's flat, Sweeney moves from the role of Agamemnon to that of Orestes, from the victim to the slayer haunted by a sense of fate. Again Eliot uses the fortune told by cards as a means of exposition which creates expectations. If the principals in the "quarrel" are left in doubt by the cards, the action centers on Sweeney and Doris with Pereira in the background. They are united by the repeated motif of paying the rent. The exposition ends with Doris's concern over the meaning of the coffin, accentuated by the knocks. These form a transition to the guests, the two Canadians and the two Americans, who provide the choruses later. Now the "good time" theme is introduced: London is too gay for the Americans, except on a visit; Sam is at home there.

Fragment of an Agon

In the "Agon" Sweeney appears and the contest begins. The "life" theme is now developed by Sweeney and Doris in a caricature of primitive love in a romantic locale. It is modulated into elemental starkness, boring to the verge of horror ("I've been born"). Then the Chorus develops the South-Sea love, with Gauguin touches, in the Aristophanic vein of caricature. Doris responds that she doesn't like eggs or life on a crocodile (not cannibal) isle. (Eggs relate to crocodiles as fertility symbols.) The Chorus then resumes the love theme, reducing it to a time sequence without responsibility. To Doris "that's not life"; she would "as soon be dead." This remark turns the dialogue to the coffin theme.

Sweeney explores the theme of life as death by means of his story and the implications of "what we gotta do." Sweeney tells his own story, for "Nobody came / And nobody went." Finally, the Chorus describes the consequence of the story as waking from a nightmare to the vengeance of the hangman. And this is one answer to Doris's question about the coffin. Again it is accentuated by knocks, but joined to the hoo-ha's which transform the fellow she once knew, "*He* could make you laugh." In this fragmentary play retribution means paying the rent, ultimately death; and since the last words of Doris and Sweeney relate this theme to Pereira, the final knocks were probably intended to introduce the unwelcome guest.

But the consequence for Sweeney is less easy to express. He finds that "When you're alone like he was alone" all relationships and identities are destroyed; life and death become meaningless distinctions. Then you discover necessity and retribution ("somebody's gotta pay the rent"). So birth as he has known it doesn't introduce you merely to copulation and death; it introduces you to necessity. When he discovered this, seeking by violence to divest himself of lust, he saw the Eumenides.

From "Sweeney Erect" to "Sweeney Among the Nightingales" to *Sweeney Agonistes,* the Sweeney myth grows in significance, in potentiality.[5] Of course he is the proper hero for a satiric melodrama based on the perception which Eliot found in Baudelaire—"that the sexual act as evil is more dignified, less boring, than as the natural, 'life-giving,' cheery automatism of the modern world." As a kind of music-hall treatment of the Avenging Deities, this libretto exploits syncopated verse and resources of the American language. The result is a masterly incorporation of serious themes into the vulgar idiom, where they draw new life from the rhythms and politesse of crude society. By way of contrast it may be recalled that "Doris's Dream Songs" in part were incorporated into "The Hollow Men."

Coriolan

Coriolan does not mark the first appearance of Coriolanus in Eliot; we may recall his presence as a hero in "A Cooking Egg" and as a figure of pride in *The Waste Land.* Here, after a "Triumphal March," he accedes to

5. See the reference to "a verse play" in *The Use of Poetry,* p. 147.

the "Difficulties of a Statesman." And here he is no more a local and temporary figure than he was before, but now he is set in scenes which qualify him partly by the caricature of enumeration, making him a qualitative figure in a quantitative world. Eliot took the first poem out of the Ariel series because, he has said, "I meant it to be the first of a sequence in the life of the character who appears in this first part as young Cyril." The central figure and young Cyril sustain a conflict in values. For Eliot's poetry the *Choruses from "The Rock"* (VI) present one of his most pointed lines (Ecclesiastes 1:9): "Do you need to be told that whatever has been, can still be?"

Triumphal March

The marching theme opens Part I (1931) in the mixed key that prevails throughout. "Stone, bronze, stone, steel"—both the ancient and the modern world are on the march. But the spectators are more important than the marchers; at least, the poem centers in their attitude. The definitive or key line is "The natural wakeful life of our Ego is a perceiving," but the source of this philosophical statement (Husserl's phenomenology) will not explain the poem. For the heart of the poem lies in the contrast between what is perceived and what is not perceived, and how this difference qualifies the perceivers with respect to life. Hence the emphasis on perception and its perquisites.

The most obvious aspect of what is perceived is the quantitative; but there is one qualitative exception, the leader. Of course there is another exception, the temple, but it attracts less attention. The climax of the quantitative aspect comes in the enumeration of the war materiel, but it is not the climax in perception. That comes with the leader, after the various groups have given another touch of caricature to this triumphal march. When the leader is seen, "There is no interrogation in his eyes" or hands; his eyes are "watchful, waiting, perceiving, indifferent." The indifference seems to negate the other qualities. Does it indicate mastery or judgment of the situation? What follows should answer the question, and this points to something hidden, ultimately "At the still point of the turning world." If this poem were *Ash-Wednesday*, it would be the Word; if later, the Light Invisible in the final chorus of *The Rock*. Here it is hidden by association with the turtle-dove, the palm, the running water; they are also associations of the Word, and certainly opposite to the eagles and trumpets; associated, rather, with peace and the Invisible Light. And, in terms of the key line, this defines the leader's attitude, pointing beyond the realm of indifference.

Hence the continuity to the temple is right, and for a triumphal march which is also Roman it must be the temple of Vesta, the temple of the eternal light. After the sacrifice, the Vestal virgins come bearing the ashes

of the dead, the "dust of dust." And then the march re-
sumes, and the parade is over.

But not the irony. Remembering the key line, and the
quantitative character of the general perception, we are
prepared for the full effect of "That is all we could see."
Then the culmination of this march is emphasized by
the ironic interpolation of the substitute for Easter Day
spent in the country; they went to church, as they came
to the parade, for the spectacle. And when "they rang
a bell," which young Cyril (the future telephone op-
erator) mistook for the bell of a street crier, that was
for him a sign of crumpets, not of the elevation of the
Holy Bread or of the "Light Invisible." Irony continues
in the careful husbandry of the sausage rather than of
the communion; and reaches its climax in the request
for a light, the great perquisite of perception as well as
of cigarettes. Only here does light have any significance
for the spectators, though its higher meaning is sug-
gested in the course of the march. As the small light
flares into "Light Light," the poem closes on a final
question, in a tongue that joins ancient and modern
Rome: "So the soldiers formed a cordon? They did." If
that brought their spectacle to an end, in the poem it
also obscures the light which is unperceived by the
spectators.

Difficulties of a Statesman

In their original context (Isaiah 40:6) the opening lines of Part II (1932) read as follows: "The voice said, Cry. And he said, What shall I cry? All flesh is grass, and all the goodliness thereof is as the flower of the field." No doubt we may expect to hear the voice and its prophet, not the crier of crumpets, in this poem. The first line combines the command and the question, but we have not gone far before we realize that the note of this cry conflicts with the practicalities of a modern statesman. Answers to the repeated question develop conflicts between desire and duty, man and station. The first answer to the question embraces, in its ironic echo of the mortality theme, the orders of vanity. The second answer represents worldly advice, presently associated with his mother; and the following proclamations reflect this advice. Here commissions for "rebuilding the fortifications" and for conference "about perpetual peace" are juxtaposed; and the Roman makers of arms appoint "a joint committee to protest against the reduction of orders." Thus the old order repeats itself. Meanwhile the guards dice on the frontiers (marches) and the frogs croak in the marshes; there is no war. But in Virgil's *Georgics* (I) the frogs foretell storms; and here the fireflies flare against the distant lightning and provoke the crucial question.

This time the answer is directed to his mother and

the family portraits, remarkably Roman, remarkably alike, lighted by the flare of torches. And his ambition, rejecting this order of vanity, turns from being "lit up" to being "hidden." The definition of this state again involves the dove and the still moment, but set high under noon's widest shadow, where the cyclamen spreads and the clematis droops, in the realm of Invisible Light. There he, "a tired head," would be, "not among these busts," with strong necks to support them, strong noses "to break the wind." He would be closer to his dead mother; perhaps, after the ceremonial of slayings, sacrifices, offerings, petitions, they may be hidden together in the peace of noon and night. Now he observes that the small creatures ("crowned with dust" in Part I) come with wing and flare, and "chirp thinly through the dust, through the night"; indeed they croak, flare, and chirp their alarm. But now as he repeats the question, it is answered by a counter-cry from the munition makers—for investigation and resignation. They form the committee of opposition and their wares dominate Part I.

If the reader has followed the reiterated images, he knows why the divided cry comes to this end, and how these images distinguish hidden spiritual values from patent worldly values. One may be permitted to believe that Virgil's plea to Vesta for peace, at the close of *Georgics I*, finds an echo in *Coriolan*.

Minor Poems

The reader should find little or no difficulty with the *Minor Poems,* and only a little more with the *Choruses from "The Rock."* If there is any difficulty, it is more likely to be found in apprehending the point of view than in understanding the text. If the first two poems under *Minor Poems* are compared with Parts II and IV of "The Hollow Men," to which they are related, the reader will perceive what themes were eliminated by their rejection and how the context for Part II was altered.

"Five-Finger Exercises" (1933) reveal a lighter side which is seen more fully in the *Old Possum's Book of Practical Cats* (1939); these wise and witty fables also provide the verbal and metrical delight of the best nonsense verse of Edward Lear. The amusing self-portrait of the last Exercise—itself inspired by Lear—is balanced by the Old Possum of his own drawing. And one might add the "Lines for an Old Man," originally for Mallarmé, since this poem is not untrue of its author when he lays "bare the tooth of wit."

The "Landscapes" (1934–35) are experiments in a more quantitative verse and in a symbolism that is used in *Four Quartets.* From each place he distils an essence which concentrates a state of mind and thus becomes accessible to a spiritual history. One is reminded that Eliot is a writer of reflective lyrics or of lyrics "sicklied o'er with the pale cast of thought," almost never of the song lyric of pure feeling—perhaps only enough to suggest the possibility. But less diluted lyric feeling emerges in occasional passages and poems, where the intellectual element is more fully submerged in the symbol, having been less analyzed.

The *Choruses from "The Rock"* (1934) present, in more explicit form and expression, themes found elsewhere in his poetry; but also experiments in choric speech modeled on Biblical patterns—perhaps influenced by the intonation of *Anabase*. To the reader these Choruses may have an accidental use in confirming or denying inferences drawn in other poems. But apart from their content they are most interesting, and most instructive for *Four Quartets*, because of their range of expression, extending the old and exploring the new, whether in metaphor, paradox, antithesis, abstract statement, or rhythmical tension. While old themes are repeated or developed, new ones are suggested or attempted. If these Choruses look both backward and forward, they are more suggestive of the future both in theme and expression, for they bring their religious feeling to bear on a wider range of life than we find in *Ash-Wednesday:*

> The desert is squeezed in the tube-train next to you . . .
> And now you live dispersed on ribbon roads . . .
> In the land of lobelias and tennis flannels.

One of Eliot's measures of poetic wit may be pointedly recalled: the poet's wealth "in shades of feeling to con-

trast and unite." Again in *Four Quartets* these contrasts
and unions are often edged, but they cut with a "sharp
compassion."

To understand the development of the *Choruses* in
expression, chiefly as it relates to *Four Quartets,* we
should turn again to the essay on Dante. For the re-
course now to imagery and now to abstract statement,
we should remember his remark about the *Paradiso:*
"The insistence throughout is upon states of feeling; the
reasoning takes only its proper place as a means of
reaching these states." [6] On the primary means, par-
ticularly as it relates to *Four Quartets,* let us recall the
remarks on Dante's realization of the Divine vision:
"Nowhere in poetry has experience so remote from
ordinary experience been expressed so concretely, by
a masterly use of that imagery of *light* which is the
form of certain types of mystical experience." [7] Here
the reader should consider the final Chorus as well as
Four Quartets. Eliot's admiration for the master's power
at every moment to "realize the inapprehensible in vis-
ual images" and his "power of establishing relations be-
tween beauty of the most diverse sorts," in language of
a peculiar lucidity, makes the poetry of Dante for him
"the one universal school of style for the writing of
poetry in any language." [8] Moreover, "Dante's 'alle-
gorical' method has great advantages for the writing of

---

6. *Selected Essays,* p. 226.
7. *Ibid.,* p. 227.
8. *Ibid.,* p. 228.

poetry: it simplifies the diction, and makes clear and precise the images"; and if their meaning as allegory need not be understood at once, "clear visual images are given much more intensity by having a meaning." [9] It must be added that these images are "in the *Inferno* most apprehensible, in the *Paradiso* most rarefied." [10] These observations help to explain the nature and range of expression, including the development toward apparent simplicity, in which the *Choruses* in some measure mediate between *Ash-Wednesday* and *Four Quartets.* Of course the *Choruses* do not develop the "allegorical method" that we find in *Four Quartets,* but they forewarn us that some of the symbols already have their meaning, though not yet their system.

---

9. *Ibid.,* p. 204.
10. *Ibid.,* p. 236.

Chapter 8

FOUR QUARTETS AND HISTORY

Four Quartets make a great lyric of history, personal but representative, exhausting the movement and meaning of time. It is a revision of Gerontion's view, a later version of "Think now History has many cunning passages." It is not a revision of the theory Eliot held then, but a deeper penetration into its meaning. In "Tradition and the Individual Talent" he had said that

. . . the historical sense involves a perception, not only of the pastness of the past, but of its presence . . . This historical sense, which is a sense of the timeless as well as of the temporal and of the timeless and of the temporal together, is what makes a writer traditional. (*Selected Essays,* p. 4.)

Thus he had thought in 1917; now he plumbs the depths of these relationships as St. Augustine explored the nature of time (*Confessions,* Bk. XI). The place names of *Four Quartets* (1943) derive their significance from this connection; it is in places that you enter into history and escape from it.

If history itself is made by time, time is made by meaning. Hear Chorus VII of *The Rock* on the Incarnation of the Word:

> Then came, at a predetermined moment, a moment in time and of time,
> A moment not out of time, but in time, in what we call history: transecting, bisecting the world of time, a moment in time but not like a moment of time,
> A moment in time but time was made through that moment: for without the meaning there is no time, and that moment of time gave the meaning.

This incarnation of the spiritual must occur in a moment of time but not resemble a moment of time. Thus the historical sense becomes or is translated into the spiritual sense. In the process another remark in "Tradition and the Individual Talent" acquires a new significance: "But the difference between the present and the past is that the conscious present is an awareness of the past in a way and to an extent which the past's awareness of itself cannot show." For the individual, this is to have had the experience but missed the meaning, to become conscious of it later. Moments of time must be in places; and the spiritual, though not of time or place, is known in time and place. The significant places for Eliot become the titles of these poems: Burnt Norton, East Coker, The Dry Salvages, and Little Gidding. From these places "in time and of time" he attempts to recover the meaning of time, but their pattern only becomes apparent in the light of moments that are "not like a moment of time." These titles make the circle of his beginning and end, from the point of family origin in England to America and return. In the cycle of being time and place change, but not the significance. If England and America meet in "Burnt Norton," Missouri and Massachusetts appear in "The Dry Salvages."

This cycle is best understood, in terms of personal history, by his remarks in a preface to *This American World* (1928) by Edgar Ansel Mowrer. First about his family. As a descendent of pioneers, of a New England family settled for two generations in Missouri, he observes,

. . . we tended to cling to places and associations as long as possible . . . with a family tendency to traditions and loyalties. . . . The family guarded jealously its connections with New England; but it was not until years of maturity that I perceived that I myself had always been a New Englander in the South West, and a South Westerner in New England; when I was sent to school in New England I lost my southern accent without ever acquiring the accent of the native Bostonian.

Then about the education of his sensibility, of which the Missouri aspect is recognizable for the first time in "The Dry Salvages":

In New England I missed the long dark river, the ailanthus trees, the flaming cardinal birds, the high limestone bluffs where we searched for fossil shellfish; in Missouri I missed the fir trees, the bay and goldenrod, the song-sparrows, the red granite and the blue sea of Massachusetts.

The New England images are probably clearest in *Ash-Wednesday*. Later he remarks that "it was perhaps easier for the grandson of pioneers to migrate eastward than it would have been for my friend (whose family had lived in the same house in the same New England seaport for two hundred and fifty years) to migrate in any direction." On the personal side, *Four Quartets* might be regarded as "a series of images of migration" which explore "time present and time past" only to collapse their meaning; or, more generally, as a series of images of history by which time is explored until it reveals the circular journey of man. The ultimate discovery is that if man enters the garden of the past and follows his history, he arrives at the garden from which he set out. But history must be interpreted by another means than time, which has already been suggested, and to which the epigraph directs us.

Burnt Norton

Fragments from Heraclitus supply the epigraph for "Burnt Norton" (1936) and translate as follows:

Although the Law of Reason (*logos*) is common, the majority of people live as though they had an understanding (wisdom) of their own.
The way upward and downward are one and the same.

With these fragments Eliot goes back to an early stage of the *Logos* doctrine which he first touched in "Mr. Eliot's Sunday Morning Service" and has since exploited in the Word. This idea of an immanent reason in the world, after being distinguished by the Stoics as Reason (*ratio*) and Word (*oratio*), was taken over by Philo and the Christian fathers. It is basic to the Gospel of St. John. Hence it will be useful to relate these fragments to the fundamental ideas of Heraclitus. For him change is the essential fact of experience, but order or harmony can be discerned. "The Many is of Sense, Unity is of Thought." This rhythm of events and order in change he explains as the reason or *logos* of the universe. "Being is intelligible only in terms of Becoming"; anything exists only in virtue of its perpetually changing relations. While fire is the ultimate term (element), unity or the One is known in order, pattern, or thought.

Now the first fragment indicates the nature of virtue, which is the subordination of the individual to the laws of harmony or the Logos, wherein freedom from change is alone to be found. The second fragment suggests that in this order or pattern opposites are merely different aspects of the same thing; paradoxes in the Many are resolved in the One. Although Eliot has turned to the philosophical background of one of the gospels, the reader may be reassured by the fact that for this framework of ideas the *Encyclopaedia Britannica* has sufficed.

In the poem, of course, time is the realm of change; the Logos belongs to the timeless, but must be known in time, and is perceived as form, or the contraries of change. Appearance and reality provide other terms for describing the two. Either ordered movement or escape from movement may indicate the Logos. If change is the essential fact of experience, and order, pattern, or harmony the chief resolver of its problems, the pattern depends upon the "still point," which returns through "Triumphal March" to the "centre of the silent Word" in *Ash-Wednesday*. Awareness of it is the chief escape from the limitations of change, but the metaphor of fire marks the essential passage from the changing to the unchanging. While the first epigraph represents virtue as subordination of the individual to this harmony, the second represents knowledge as comprehension of the pattern which reconciles contraries. Thus Heraclitus has provided the poem with basic ideas that have analogues in both Christian and Hindu thought, in St. John of the Cross or the *Bhagavad-Gita*, subsuming material no less different than Christian mysticism and the appearance of history. In consequence *Four Quartets* is Eliot's most philosophical poem or sequence, and its method of subsumptive ideas is most reminiscent of *The Waste Land*, eliciting deeper significance from memory and desire.

I

The opening of "Burnt Norton"—named after a Gloucestershire manor but suggestive of his American

"Landscapes"—is an example of the use of abstract thought to lead to a state of mind, a method which Eliot observed in Dante. Here he collapses the divisions of time, giving us the eternal presence of all time, or the aspect of eternity.[1] But this collapse has consequences: "all time is unredeemable," for redemption depends upon the differences in time; what might have been remains possible only in thought.[2] Yet the unrealized and the realized aspects of the past point to the same end when all time is collapsed into the present. And memory or the mind includes both aspects of the past, both the unrealized and the realized. Thus his words can raise echoes in the reader, who has had similar experience. But to what purpose he disturbs the souvenirs of past desires or elusive experiences he is unaware. Yet he is breaking the bonds of time and place discovered in the beginning of *Ash-Wednesday.*

Other echoes besides the footfalls inhabit the "rose-garden," which has become associated with "what might have been." And he can invite the reader, who is now his fellow, to follow them. The bird as a subjective symbol is not new in Eliot, and quickness is of the essence of the bird and of seizing elusive experiences (see "Cape Ann"). The bird acts as if in a game, introducing us to the childish vision which "confounds the actual and the fanciful"—here used to con-

---

1. In Plato's *Timaeus* time is "a moving likeness of eternity."
2. The pressure of Ecclesiastes (here 3:15) upon Eliot's mind has been incisive.

vey something real and yet not real, unrealized desire or experience. To "follow the deception of the thrush" into this first world, which resembles that of "New Hampshire," is to follow the maneuvers by which the thrush confuses reality and illusion, as in *The Waste Land*. In the description of this garden the center of its meaning is found in the antitheses and paradoxes of the heard and the unheard, the seen and the unseen, the contradictory sense of something experienced and something missed. This reaches its climax in the illusion of water created by sunlight in the dry pool and the lotus rising silently. Then a cloud empties the pool. At this juncture, evidently a moment of potential discovery—note the imagery of the children "hidden excitedly"—the bird again becomes directive, even solicitous. What is missed is indicated by the bird's reason (an echo of *Murder in the Cathedral*): "human kind Cannot bear very much reality." Illusion is apparently more congenial. Again past and future, possibility and realization, ambiguously "Point to one end, which is always present." Is this the moment of real perception where the pattern of time is found? an approach to what is later called plenitude? Certainly the real is something more than the realized in the garden, for its potentiality remains hidden.[3] The identity discovered in this collapse of time is also found in the eternal cycle of Ecclesiastes (1).

---

3. Mr. Theodore Silverstein suggests a source for this garden in "The Looking Glass" by Walter de la Mare.

II

The next section begins by collapsing many dispa-
rates into a common pattern; from the buried axle-tree
to the wheel of the stars many opposites are reconciled
by the eternal pattern, the dance of the turning world.
These opposites, presented in correspondences of the
microcosm and macrocosm, are reconciled in both
realms by the center of the wheel.

After these images, abstractions take up the task of
defining the center of this unchanging pattern, "the
still point"; and this is defined by negatives of all that
appears to belong to "the turning world." Yet if it were
not for this point, "There would be no dance, and there
is only the dance." This of course asserts the basic ideas
of Heraclitus, both change and pattern. As this percep-
tion relates to the *Logos,* it cannot be related to time
and place, but the perception is none the less real.

At least he can say what it was. It is the experience
of what he presently calls "plenitude." Again paradoxes
define this sense of release and fulfilment, of the com-
pletion of the partially apprehended, both the ecstasy
and the horror of life.[4] Yet the chains of time past and
future woven in the changing body protect man from
such full-eyed views of "heaven and damnation, Which
flesh cannot endure." Past and future allow him but a
little consciousness; the mind aware of itself is not

---

4. *Erhebung:* exaltation.

aware of objects that belong to time; time is an escape from consciousness. Though consciousness does not belong to time, it is only in time that significant moments like that in the rose-garden can be remembered. Thus the moment out of time, the timeless moment, is involved in time; and time must be conquered through time. It will be noticed that the past and future, not the present, are the special enemies of, or releases from, consciousness.

III

In contrast to "*there* we have been" the poem now develops the "here." It is "a place of disaffection" because it belongs to the time before and after such moments. It is "in a dim light" because it has neither the daylight of plenitude nor the darkness of vacancy, the two ways of escaping the limitations of the temporal. There is "only a flicker" of light over "strained time-ridden faces" in this subway world, with its belching "of unhealthy souls Into the faded air." Though dim, "this twittering world" lacks the cleansing darkness.

For this darkness one must descend lower than this subway world, to the world of internal darkness and solitude, the vacancy which is the negation or elimination of this world. This is the other way, the "dark night" of the mystics; down, not up as in the way of plenitude; in mysticism they are the positive and negative ways of knowledge and ignorance. But they are

alike in "abstention from movement," which would
bring them into the realm of time, where the world
moves in desire—by an appropriate subway metaphor.
Thus in the conquest of the temporal, of change, the
ways down to the axle-tree and up to the stars are
one and the same.

IV

But our darkness is like death. Time has buried the
day, not emptied the sensual or cleansed affection; has
destroyed plenitude without bringing vacancy. In this
darkness will the flowers that respond only to the sun
turn down to us? Will the yew cover us? Desire will
not die. The answer also involves the response to light,
for after the vibrating wing of the kingfisher "has an-
swered light to light, and is silent," the light remains
"at the still point," though nothing reflects it. Thus
the paradox of the unmoving and the moving still gov-
erns "the turning world." But in this inversion of the
rose-garden (the key experience in the key symbols)
the cloud becomes more comprehensive, time and death
extend its negation. Yet a bird still points to reality.

V

The problem of time and the temporal—the constant
problem of the poem—now moves into the realm of art.
Words and music move only in time, and hence have

the limitation of death. They can only reach the unchanging state, "the stillness," by form or pattern, as the detail of a Chinese jar moves perpetually in its unchanging pattern. The problem of unchanging unity is pursued with the violin, again attempting to rise above the limitations of time, where "all is always now." The temporal arts provide the hardest test for his conclusion that "only through time time is conquered." Likewise words fail under the burden of meaning, fall out of order, do not achieve the stillness of form. Here it becomes obvious that "stillness" involves both lack of sound and lack of movement. Moreover, the failure of words obviously moves in the moral as well as the esthetic realm. Their tendency to say things other than those required of them is treated as temptation; here "word" with a small letter moves into relation with the capitalized Word, and the special "voices of temptation" are grief or sorrow, foolish or delusive fancy. If we are startled by the apparent paradox of "the funeral dance," let us remember that "there is only the dance." The dance of death suggests a Heraclitean resolution of change and constancy.

"The detail of the pattern is movement"—this is the solution already suggested, as in the Chinese jar. Now it is given another relationship, "As in the figure of the ten stairs," the ladder of ascent to union with God for St. John of the Cross. This relationship not only objectifies "pattern" and "detail" but leads into the distinction between desire and love, which is again that between the moving and the unmoving. Desire is movement, not an end in itself; love is not movement, but "the cause and end of movement." Love is timeless, and only appears as desire when caught in the aspect of time, the realm of Becoming, not of Being. Thus desire may lead to love, movement to stillness, and the conquest of time through time is achieved. Then "Sudden in a shaft of sunlight" comes the illumination of the moment in the rose-garden, and he knows why he disturbed "the dust on a bowl of rose-leaves." Now he repeats the injunction to be "quick" and asserts that the moment is "here, now, always." The conclusion emphasizes the culpable past and future which in the poem prevent the realization of such moments, and thus we understand why the poem begins by collapsing time into the present, a semblance of eternity. It is only in this aspect that time can find its pattern or meaning, which has been suggested in love. This exploration of experience seeks to know the timeless in time, to escape from movement to stillness; to conquer the limitations of time, its perpetual movement and change; to see things in the aspect of eternity, where love escapes the limitation of desire.

East Coker

"East Coker" (1940), named for the place of family origin, continues to explore the relations of time to change and constancy, with particular reference to personal history. The order of time and change has a rhythm which leads to the conclusion that "in my beginning is my end"; but this collapse of the relations of time makes possible another conclusion, that "in my end is my beginning." In the pattern of stillness it can even be said "that the end precedes the beginning." In the succession of time there is the cycle of life and death in which matter perpetually changes form; if what lives must die, what dies is not lost, and there is a time for both. (See Ecclesiastes, 1.)

Thus a beginning commits one to an end. And the afternoon scene is made to project this sense of the end by details which suggest the departure of light and the approach of night.

In what is now an open field, if set in the proper perspective, you can perceive its buried life; and what you will see is the dance of life. The dancing passage draws upon an ancestor, Sir Thomas Elyot in *The Governour* (I. 21). Round and round or leaping through the fire—for desire becomes the Heraclitean fire—they keep time, keep the rhythm of life, which ends in "dung and death." (See Ecclesiastes, 3.)

If "another day" is always suggestive, it is limited here by "prepares for heat and silence," which of course has significance beyond the local scene.[5] Fire, which gives both heat and light, remains a basic element or a metaphor of desire. The speaker is localized only by

---

5. "Dawn points": see "the point of dawn" in Milton's "Nativity Hymn."

being in his beginning, its real place is left indecisive. While it is impossible to translate the qualities of the emotion or the associated feelings of image or metaphor, it is necessary to perceive the ideological basis if they are to make a coherent impact.

II

The opening question continues the problem of beginning and end: not only in the concern of late November with spring or summer, but in their confusion; note how their products or effects are juxtaposed or mingled. The heavenly wars or storms involve astronomical phenomena that belong to November (Scorpion and Leonids) and herald the fire that will precede the return of the ice-cap to the earth. It should be noticed that Heraclitean fire has become insistent, and thus far destructive.

This periphrastic style, in which one must be alert to ideas that govern the circumlocution of images, is now rejected for more direct expression of the feeling. November—to continue the other style—has not brought what "the disturbance of the spring" looked forward to, the autumnal serenity and wisdom. Is this reputed wisdom a deception, even a self-deception on the part of age? Is the serenity a deliberate obtuseness, the wisdom dead or useless in the darkness observed or shunned? At best, experience brings a knowledge of limited value, for on the changing pattern of things it imposes an old pattern. In terms of the essay which I quoted at the beginning, "the conscious present is an awareness of the past in a way and to an extent which the past's awareness of itself cannot show"; and in terms of the individual, it is "a new and shocking" awareness of what we have been. If we are undeceived by time, it is from deceptions that no longer harm. If we are misled, like Dante at the outset of the *Inferno*, the fancy of man remains incorrigible; it is always lighting where there is no secure foothold, always risking delusion.[6] The wisdom of age is folly, fear of reality, "fear of fear and frenzy . . . fear of possession" by another. There is no wisdom in age, only in humility, which is not limited. But the houses and dancers are limited by the temporal order. Now an echo of Tennyson passes into an echo of Milton.

III

And into the darkness of this order, which the old either peer into or shun, they all go, all the eminent persons. It is the subway or deadened world again, but elevated to "the vacant interstellar spaces," and thus "cold the sense and lost the motive of action."[7] But the darkness which the speaker would accept in humility is the darkness of God, the way of negation and ignorance. The three-fold simile marks stages in the

6. "grimpen": mire or bog.
7. *Almanach de Gotha*: a kind of genealogical almanac of the world.

acceptance: consciousness of what is being taken away, consciousness of the emptiness left, consciousness of nothing but conciousness; from theatre to subway to ether. Without hope, love, even faith, the soul must wait, for they are all in the waiting; and the soul is not ready for thought. If accepted thus, the darkness shall become the light and the inactivity the dancing; the "interstellar spaces" will lose their effect.

The sense of this becoming is conveyed by the images which follow, chiefly a presence of things unseen, reminiscent of the rose-garden, and "pointing to the agony" of rebirth.

This is followed by a conscious repetition of the negative way, set forth in all the paradoxes which characterize its discovery of reality.

IV

But the ultimate cure of rebirth depends upon the wounded surgeon, Christ, whose compassion is "sharp." As the dying nurse the Church reminds us that the agony of dying is necessary to rebirth. But the perversity of Adam "the ruined millionaire" has endowed our hospital, the earth, so that "if we do well" we must share his ruin in a negative benefit. The mortal chill creeps up the body, and if we are to be restored the fever must be resolved in fires that make us freeze and quake, that are desirable in their flame, painful in their smoke. The suffering of the "bleeding hands" is our only food and drink if we are to recover, but in spite of this we consider ourselves healthy, and even call "this Friday good." The redeeming fire, by which desire can be transformed into love, has now appeared.

V

Here the speaker confronts himself in "the silent funeral," after twenty years spent in "trying to learn to use words," largely wasted in different kinds of failure, each "a raid on the inarticulate" feelings. While the ultimate discoveries have been made, they must be made again and again, and now under unfavorable conditions.[8] "For us, there is only the trying." The speaker is most aware of the emulation of Dante.

And thus to try again. Home is the place from which we start; years only make the world stranger, its "pattern more complicated" by dead and living. It is not the intense moment, set apart from past and future, "but a lifetime burning in every moment," not only of one man but of his ancestors. There is a time for youth, and a time for age, looking over the past; but "love is most nearly itself" when place and time cease to matter. "Old men ought to be explorers," like Ulysses —but that of Dante rather than of Tennyson, both "still and still moving" into a deeper realization of the ultimate. Then "through the dark cold and the empty deso-

8. "One of the unhappy necessities of human experience," Eliot had said in 1930, "is that we have to 'find things out for ourselves.'"

lation," they may perceive that "in my end is my beginning," that home is also what one comes to.

The Dry Salvages

"The Dry Salvages" (1941), named for a small group of rocks off the coast of Cape Ann, involves a conversion, by their beacon, of *les trois sauvages* into saviors from the peril of wreckage. But they belong to the category of gods with which the poem begins. The "strong brown god," the river which the poet knew in Missouri, is a destroyer; he is time, and his rhythm runs through the nursery and the Missouri scene from spring to winter.

"The river is within us, the sea is all about us"—for the river is man's time, the microcosmic rhythm of life, but the sea is the earth's time, the macrocosmic rhythm of eternity; both are frontiers. The sea, a witness to "earlier and other creation," thus has "many gods and many voices." And it affects the land, for its "salt is on the briar rose," its "fog is in the fir trees." Its voices are not only numerous but varied in meaning; under its fog the tolling bell rung by the ground swell "measures time not our time"; as worried women lie awake trying to fathom man's time, earth's time "clangs the bell."

II

"Where is there an end" to time's "soundless wailing" and "silent withering" and "drifting wreckage"? To the "prayer of the bone on the beach"—the prayer that cannot be prayed at the announcement of disaster?

"There is no end," only more of it—adding the emotionless years of disillusion, adding "the failing Pride or resentment at failing powers" and "the unattached devotion" and the silent listening to the sound of the last annunciation.

"Where is the end" of the fishermen? But "a time that is oceanless" or an ocean without wreckage or a future certain of its destination is unthinkable.

"We have to think of them as forever" about their business, not as making unpayable trips for worthless hauls.

"There is no end of it," no end "to the movement of pain" that is itself "painless and motionless," to "the bone's prayer to Death its God." There is only the "barely prayable Prayer of the one Annunciation" of life to man. The opening sestina becomes functional in its projection of the pattern of things.

As one grows older the past assumes another pattern, neither a sequence nor a development. The latter is a partial fallacy which becomes "a means of disowning the past." The moments of sudden illumination, in which we missed the meaning, are restored in a different form by an approach to the meaning. And the past revived in the meaning is the experience of many generations, probably including some pre-historical memories. But we discover that the moments of agony are also permanent, though this fact is better appreciated vicariously, since "our own past is covered by the currents of action." Thus time the destroyer is also time the preserver; and both the river and the rocks in the sea illustrate it, not to mention the bitterness that remains the bite in the apple. For *les trois sauvages,* now the warning "salvages," perpetuate the first wreck of man.

III

This paradox of time seems to be Krishna's meaning; [9] and it may be put thus: That the future is a faded flower of regret "for those who are not yet here to regret," pressed between the yellowed leaves of an unopened book. Krishna adds meaning to the paradox that "the way up is the way down, the way forward is the way back." But "time is no healer," for the patient changes with time. In the journey and the voyage the passengers do not belong to constancy and the passage to time, but both belong to change. Time is not an escape. But during the voyage, while time seems to be withdrawn, you can be indifferent to past and future. And in the moment of contemplation you can receive

9. See *Bhagavad-Gita;* for example, the Second and Eighth Lesson.

the teaching of Krishna: [10] that the object of contempla-
tion determines the succession of being, or comes to
fruition in the following being; but this action must be
free from self-interest. By the teaching of Krishna this
contemplated "sphere of being" is the real destination
of the voyagers. Hence there can be no "fare well,"
only "fare forward."

IV

But all those concerned with the sea of time need
assistance. Hence the Virgin, whose shrine stands ap-
propriately on the promontory, is invoked to pray for
those whose business carries them to sea, for the women
who wait at home, and for those who do not return.
Figlia del tuo figlio (*Paradiso* 33:1), "daughter of thy
son," pray for those whom the tolling of the ground
swell cannot reach—the perpetual call to devotion. One
scarcely needs to observe in this poem the admonition
of the flowing river within us and the sea all about us.

V

From the true means of succor, this section turns to
an inventory of all the modern means of reading the
past and the future. While such practices are stimulated
by the "distress of nations," men's curiosity "clings to
that dimension," the dimension of time. It is given only

---

10. See *Bhagavad-Gita*, Eighth Lesson.

to the saint "to apprehend The point of intersection of the timeless With time"; for the rest of us there is only "the moment in and out of time," the unattended moment, now imaged by most of the images that have been used to project it. To such "hints followed by guesses" must be added "prayer, observance, discipline, thought and action." This "hint half guessed" is the incarnation of the timeless in time, the reconciliation of being and becoming, for men who are otherwise driven by underworld powers. Right action also requires freedom from past and future, but for most of us this is realized only in continuing to try to attain it. We must be content at the last if our return of the physical to time nourishes (not too far from the tree of the church or nurse) "the life of significant soil," such as that of "East Coker."

Little Gidding

Little Gidding, a place of the yew-tree, is remembered as the Anglican religious community founded by Nicholas Ferrar and visited by poets like George Herbert and Richard Crashaw. In the poem of this name (1942) the earlier "winter lightning" becomes a paradoxical season which collapses winter and spring. It is what Donne called St. Lucy's day, the shortest day of the year; here its brightness becomes intense by contrast, "like pentecostal fire In the dark time of the year." It is a proper season to alleviate the sickness of man in

Part IV of "East Coker." While it is "the spring time," it is neither in "time's covenant" nor "in the scheme of generation." Like the moment of sudden illumination, it belongs to the timeless covenant; and in temporal terms could only be consummated by "Zero summer."

"If you came this way in May time," by your probable route from your probable place, the hedgerow would be white again, but with voluptuary sweetness. In this modern journey of the Magi—for the "broken king" is Charles I—the end of the journey, regardless of your state of mind, would be the same: "the dull façade and the tombstone" or "a husk of meaning" known only in fulfilment; and even for those with purpose, the purpose "is altered in fulfilment." Of all places which "are the world's end . . . this is the nearest, in place and time." In Little Gidding the explicit end is more obvious than the implicit spiritual end.

If you came this way by any route from anywhere at any time, "it would always be the same," requiring that you "put off Sense and notion." For "You are here to kneel," and prayer is beyond them. Here, "where prayer has been valid," you are to communicate with the dead; this is "the intersection of the timeless moment," both in and out of place and time.

II

And this is what you can learn from the dead. In the general dissolution, by the passions into the elements, that the death of air is "the death of hope and despair"; that the death of earth "laughs without mirth"; that the death of water and fire rots what we forget. The impact of the war now becomes obvious in the poem; but it belongs to the essence, not to the accidents, and nowhere more than when the dove unites the "pentecostal fire" and the dive-bomber.

The experience of the fire warden now makes a time that is often critical in Eliot's poetry even more critical. The before-dawn watch, after the dove-bomber has passed, brings further instruction from the dead. Meeting the "familiar compound ghost" with "the brown baked features," he realizes another experience of the "intersection time." This ghost, as his features indicate, is a purgatorial figure compounded out of such dead masters as Dante, to whom he listens as he walks in a "dead" patrol. This purgatorial spirit has found an easy passage to this world, now become much like his own. Saying that their mutual concern was speech—here he reminds us, though in words of Mallarmé, of Dante and the function of the poet—

> To purify the dialect of the tribe
> And urge the mind to aftersight and foresight,

he discloses "the gifts reserved for age." First, "the cold friction of expiring sense" (compare "Gerontion"); second, "the conscious impotence of rage At human folly"; last, "the rending pain of re-enactment Of all that you have done, and been." There is no escape from this circle,

> unless restored by that refining fire
> Where you must move in measure, like a dancer.

Thus Heraclitean fire becomes purgatorial when it is made significant by pattern or discipline, and thus experience may be refined. In this fire Dante placed Arnaut Daniel, whom he honored. The ghost fades on the blowing of the "all-clear." It should be observed that the circle appears in *Four Quartets* both as a form of limitation and as a form of release.

III

As the speaker takes up the theme of the dead or history, this year's words acquire another voice. Three conditions, often similar in appearance, must be distinguished: attachment to self, things, and persons; detachment from them; and indifference to them. The latter resembles death, and grows between "the live and the dead nettle" of desire. Echoes of Krishna may be heard in this voice. The use of memory or history is for liberation, for expanding love beyond desire, "and so liberation From the future as well as the past." In *Four Quartets* memory has tied us to the past and desire to the future. If love of a country begins as a form of personal attachment, it comes to find the personal, not indifferent, but of little importance. Thus history

may be both servitude and freedom. By this perception
the past is transfigured into another pattern.

With Juliana of Norwich one can now say, "Sin is
Behovely," that is, incumbent; "but all shall be well." [11]
And "the faces and places" return in a new pattern. He
thinks of Little Gidding and the Civil Wars, of their
people now "united in the strife which divided them";
he thinks of Charles I coming to Little Gidding; of
men like Strafford, Laud, and Charles on the scaffold;
of Milton, "who died blind and quiet," and is echoed in
"East Coker." If any should ask why these dead men
should be celebrated more than the dying, "It is not
to ring the bell backward." Nor is it (by Sir Thomas
Browne) to "raise up the ghost of a Rose" of civil fac-
tion; we cannot "follow an antique drum." It is be-
cause these rivals "accept the constitution of silence,"
of detachment; from the defeated too we inherit "what
they had to leave us"—a symbol of moral action per-
fected in death. And all shall be well by a similar purifi-
cation of motive "in the ground of our beseeching."

IV

Here the dove, the propitious form of the pentecostal
dive-bomber, breaks the air with "the only hope" from
despair, redemption "from fire by fire." Compare Acts
2:1-4.

---

11. See G. E. Hodgson, *English Mystics;* E. I. Watkin, *The English
Way.*

"Love is the unfamiliar Name" that devised the torment and gave "the wounded surgeon," who can remove the Nessus "shirt of flame." We only live consumed by the fire of desire or the fire of love, the fire of becoming or the fire of being. Whether with Heraclitus or Lear, we are "bound Upon a wheel of fire."

V

For man becoming is a cycle of actions which are both ends and beginnings; we start from the end and arrive at the beginning. In the verbal art every phrase in its pattern is both an end and a beginning. Likewise, any action is an end, a death, and a beginning. Thus we die with the dying and are born with the dead; for we die in action or movement and revive in its meaning. The moment of desire and the moment of grief are of equal duration. History or memory, in which these moments are known, should be a liberation from time.

> A people without history
> Is not redeemed from time, for history is a pattern
> Of timeless moments.

So in a chapel at Little Gidding "History is now and England," a moment in time but also out of time; for the dead, in their detachment from time, reveal the pattern of movement, both the cause and end of desire.

"With the drawing of this Love and the voice of this Calling"—the call of "the unfamiliar Name" from *The*

Cloud of Unknowing— [12] this conclusion extends the
final theme of "East Coker."

The end of our never ceasing exploration will be to
arrive at the beginning "and know the place for the
first time"—"through the unknown, remembered gate"
of the Garden; "at the source of the longest river" in
man, where the voices were half-heard "between two
waves of the sea." This, the ultimate form of the garden
entered in "Burnt Norton," is the end which was also
the beginning. To the former injunction to be quick,
there is now added "A condition of complete sim-
plicity," requiring the original innocence, the ultimate
reversion. Then all shall be well when the pentecostal
tongues of flame are folded into the interwoven knot of
fire, when the fire of love and the rose of desire are
one. [13] Thus, as with Heraclitus, fire becomes the ul-
timate metaphor or translation from the realm of be-
coming to the realm of being; or with Dante, the
universal form of love seen at the close of the *Paradiso*.
If we remember the burning of "The Fire Sermon," we
can now understand into what it might have been re-
solved. For this is the end of the garden myth that
began unconsciously in "La Figlia Che Piange."

In thus searching the meaning of history for the
meaning of life Eliot has never been far from those

---

12. *Ibid.* Compare the wheel in *Paradiso* 1:76-78.
13. A crowned knot (Naut.) is a knot finished by interweaving the
strands so as to prevent untwisting. This "crowned knot" connects the
spiritual consummation of the *Paradiso* (C. 33) with the sea, as in *Para-
diso* 3:85-87.

doctrines of Heraclitus which relate the earliest stages
of European thought to the fundamental principles of
Buddhism. From such ideas as "while we live our souls
are dead within us, but when we die our souls are re-
stored to life," it can be concluded that for Heraclitus
"knowledge of the self is one with knowledge of the
Universal Logos (Reason); such knowledge is the basis
not only of conduct but of existence itself in its only
real sense." How such ideas have been employed, or
the kindred ideas that have been assimilated to them,
in translating Eliot's historical sense into his spiritual
sense must be determined by the poems themselves;
but the application is sufficiently general to warrant
the extension of the epigraphs for "Burnt Norton" to
the whole sequence, in which the paradoxes of expe-
rience are resolved in a higher order. For history "with-
out the meaning there is no time"; and with the mean-
ing, it is timeless. In subordinating the individual mind
to the Logos of history, he is also deepening his earlier
awareness that "the mind of Europe—the mind of his
own country—a mind which he learns in time to be
much more important than his own private mind—is
a mind which changes, and that this change is a de-
velopment which abandons nothing *en route*." [14]

Thus the pattern of history supplies the pattern of
life, the meaning of history the meaning of life. But
the Incarnation of the Word provides the key to both:

14. *Selected Essays*, p. 6.

A moment not out of time, but in time, in what we call
  history: transecting, bisecting the world of time, a mo-
  ment in time but not like a moment of time,
A moment in time but time was made through that
  moment: for without the meaning there is no time, and
  that moment of time gave the meaning.

In the order of history and in the order of life the
meaning is the same. The *Logos* of being appears in
the paradoxes of becoming; and for Heraclitus, Krishna,
or Donne, it can be said,

> As West and East
> In all flatt Maps (and I am one) are one,
> So death doth touch the Resurrection.

As in *Ash-Wednesday*, love is the great resolver of these
paradoxes—the higher love which in *The Waste Land*
could not rise out of the lower. This resolution is em-
phasized by the fact that it grows out of the same
external form. The sequence of time becomes a circle
in the timeless realm, but the flux of the former serves
to reveal the emotional form of the latter; the succes-
sion of desire is resolved in the continuum of love.

Here correspondences to the circle, such as the cycle
of the seasons or the elements, are not factitious devices
of form. Superficially the correspondences, repeated
themes, and resolutions suggest a musical structure,
but fundamentally they embody the ideological form,
which in the wheel of becoming connects Heraclitus
with the view of time in Plato's *Timaeus*. Commenting
on the latter, Cornford observes a contrast that is rele-

vant to the tradition of *Four Quartets:* the Greek thought of the movement of time as circular, but Locke thought of it as rectilinear. Now Eliot concludes, against Gerontion, that in history the pattern or timeless form of life is realized and may be discerned.

Chapter 9

POSTSCRIPT

Since *Four Quartets* involve the question of artistic form in their more general problem, it will be appropriate to conclude with some observations that relate to its solution by Eliot. In his essay on Dante in *The Sacred Wood* he distinguishes between the framework and the form of a poem. In Dante the framework is the allegory; the emotional form is something different, but a "structure made possible by the scaffold." For "this structure is an ordered scale of human emotions," and the framework or scaffold provides the order. Thus the artistic emotion presented by any episode is dependent upon the whole order provided by this external or obvious structure. Dante, as opposed to Shakespeare, "does not analyse the emotion so much as he exhibits its relation to other emotions." For this structure of emotions his allegory is the necessary scaffold—is the objective correlative. It enables him to state a vision, to state his thought and feeling "in terms of something *perceived*."

In a similar way a "character" for Eliot becomes a symbol of emotion, and his situation or circumstances the framework in which the emotion exhibits its relation to other feelings, and thus acquires its significance. Ideas as such seldom enter Eliot's poetry, but become imaginative experiences or states of mind; experiences do not verify thoughts, but project, animate, or sanction them. If the emotions are not analyzed into thoughts, they are exhibited in terms capable of being translated into thoughts, and hence yield to understanding or interpretation. One of the most striking aspects of his framework is the historical, yet it belongs to the character of his vision. For him, as we have seen, the historical sense is a sense of the changing and the permanent which sharpens the perception of both and makes one aware of their simultaneous existence. Of course the historical aspect, as a form of imaginative extension, is used to exhibit the relations of feeling. And for Eliot this method of exhibiting rather than analyzing emotion assimilates Dante to the Symbolists, but it is not all that brings them together. There is a metaphysical as well as historical extension of experience.

In a "Note sur Mallarmé et Poe," published in 1926,[1] he distinguishes between the "metaphysical" and the philosophical poet chiefly by their belief in the theories which they employ or invent. The Metaphysical poets —here Donne, Poe, and Mallarmé—are not committed to belief:

---

1. See *La Nouvelle Revue Française,* vol. 27, pp. 524-26.

They make use of their theories in order to attain a more limited and more exclusive end: in order to refine and to develop their power of sensibility and emotion. Their work was an expansion of their sensibility beyond the limits of the normal world, a discovery of new objects proper to excite new feelings.

They are distinguished from hallucinative poets because "they do not leap abruptly into a dream world." With Mallarmé, Donne, Baudelaire, or even Poe,

we are in a world in which all the material, all the data, are perfectly familiar to us; only by each of these poets our sensibility is extended; from which it follows that the development, being continuous, remains perfectly real.

In these terms *The Waste Land* is a Metaphysical poem; yet all of Eliot's major poems have this visionary quality, and his conceptual metaphors constantly extend our sensibility. Both Metaphysical and philosophical poetry are found in Dante; and Metaphysical poets, when they excel, have the speculative turn of mind: "for example, Cavalcanti, Donne, Poe, and Mallarmé." By introducing metaphysical ideas or abstractions into a world of familiar objects, such poets extend our feeling for those objects, modify the common by association with the strange, refine and develop our sensibility or perception. Their poetry is not a complete reorganization of the normal world, but rather an extension of it—a development of some aspects of the physical world into the metaphysical world. Thus they achieve "a simplification of current life into something rich and strange." These observations help to describe certain aspects of

Eliot's poetry, and to intimate the extent to which it
is, in his own terms, Metaphysical poetry. From first
to last there has been no change in the basic character
of his poetry, except as he has striven, especially in
Four Quartets, "to get *beyond poetry,* as Beethoven,
in his later works, strove to get *beyond music*"; [2] or, in
other words, to achieve the discipline of Ben Jonson
and Marianne Moore.

To a large extent his imagery, though often not Meta-
physical in precisely this sense, has contributed to
similar effects—as it did in Donne—by startling associa-
tions or simplifications. Although Donne passed easily
from microcosmic to macrocosmic imagery, so has Eliot.
If Donne did much with "a rag and a bone and a hank
of hair," Eliot's imagery has been equally striking, per-
haps equally circumscribed. Yet this restriction should
not be regarded as barren repetition, but rather as the
plumbing of deeper and more complex levels of the
same or similar feeling. It is questionable whether there
is a radical change of attitude or area of emotion with-
out an equal change in imagery. But his is largely a
development in depth, hence intensive rather than ex-
tensive in effect. Consider the areas of imagery which
he has cultivated. For example, in the early urban
imagery there is mingled both natural and literary
stock, including Biblical; at first these explore ironic
feeling, develop mock-heroic effects; presently the im-
agery of nursery rhymes is added to similar effect; and

---

2. See Matthiessen's *Achievement of T. S. Eliot,* Chap. IV.

then all are raised to a much greater intensity. There
is also a development from indirection to the more
direct, as if a latent feeling at last dared to stand clear,
or could be defined. It is most significant that at no
stage has Dante failed to supply Eliot with means to
explore his feeling. At the center of his development
has been the Arnaut Daniel passage, where the better
craftsman sings in the topmost circle of flame.

The doctrine of impersonality—assumed not only for
theoretical reasons but also by a reticence bound to the
slow accretions of experience—has issued in dramatic
projection by various masks or characters and in ironic
or paradoxical expression. These are both an escape
from personality and the necessary mode of a complex
personality. They provide both imaginative release and
transcendence of emotion, but they are adjuncts of
the doctrine. For this has always meant the belief he
ascribed to Dante, that the experiences found in poetry
must be important, not because they happened to a
certain person, but "important in themselves." Their
poetic values are not accidents of the personal voice,
even when this is undisguised.

Though on this score he has found in Donne some
impurity of motive, Eliot, like Donne, has made a new
music, a new beauty, a new order of feeling, which
many people still deny and take for their opposites.
Others perceive them but reject their significance be-
cause they find his religion an escape. It is truer to
say that without his religious sense, which was always

there, he could not have seen and expressed so power-
fully that which these critics find him evading. For if
religion is illusion, it first makes its victim aware—in
his own words—of "the bottom of the abyss," as in
Greek tragedy; those who have never seen "that awful
mystery" do not need illusion. But that the vision is
there, most of his critics admit, and more is not re-
quired of poetry. His later poetry, though a Christian
integration, embraces conflicts that widen its emotional
impact and extend its experience of life. But doubt is
overcome by belief and the naïve imagery has lost its
ironic ambiguity. Still, in the humanistic tradition, Eliot
explores, extends, and preserves those perceptions and
values that have been memorable for mankind.

"Certainly," if I may repeat what I wrote more than
twenty years ago, "the echoes of Dante and Baudelaire
are not accidents in *The Waste Land,* which places
Eliot in the ranks of those who have created visions of
their age." Whether or not you like what he makes
you see, he has given form to some of the most signifi-
cant feeling of our time. For he has been "able to see
beneath both beauty and ugliness; to see the boredom,
and the horror, and the glory." His vision of glory is
defined by a remark which he made in 1930: "It is true
to say that the glory of man is his capacity for salva-
tion; it is also true to say that his glory is his capacity
for damnation." For him Dante has revealed the first
capacity and Baudelaire the second. His own sense of
glory is realized more completely in *Four Quartets*

than in his prose "Defense of the Islands," which com-
memorates the time of trial:

Let these memorials of built stone—music's enduring instru-
ment, of many centuries of patient cultivation of the earth, of
English verse

be joined with the memory of this defense of the islands

and the memory of those appointed to the grey ships—battle-
ship, merchantman, trawler—contributing their share to the
ages' pavement of British bone on the sea floor

and of those who, in man's newest form of gamble with death,
fight the power of darkness in air and fire

and of those who have followed their forebears to Flanders
and France, those undefeated in defeat, unalterable in tri-
umph, changing nothing of their ancestors' ways but the
weapons

and those again for whom the paths of glory are the lanes and
the streets of Britain:

to say, to the past and the future generations of our kin and of
our speech, that we took up our positions, in obedience to
instructions.

T. S. ELIOT
9. vi. 40

(Reprinted by permission from *Britain at War,* Museum of Modern
Art: New York, 1941.)

BIBLIOGRAPHICAL NOTE

A useful *Bibliographical Check-List of the Writings of T. S. Eliot* has been provided by D. C. Gallup. The best general criticism of Eliot's poetry will be found in F. O. Matthiessen's *Achievement of T. S. Eliot.* This work also brings together a good deal of special information; and more on the epigraphs is furnished by Jane Worthington in *American Literature* for March 1949. Leonard Unger's *T. S. Eliot: A Selected Critique,* which includes a bibliography, supplies an introduction to the corpus of Eliot criticism, leaning to the sophisticated. On the nature of his poetry Eliot himself has spoken with most authority, but mainly in critical essays on other poets. In this book the references are chiefly to *The Sacred Wood* (1920), *Selected Essays* (1932), *The Use of Poetry and the Use of Criticism* (1933), for which the American editions have been used.

More recent criticism of Eliot will be found in *T. S. Eliot: The Design of his Poetry* by Elizabeth Drew;

The Art of T. S. Eliot by Helen Gardner; *Poetry and Belief in the Work of T. S. Eliot* by Kristian Smidt. On the general background of ideas see Smidt's book and H. V. Routh's *English Literature and Ideas in the Twentieth Century.*